PUT YOUR
MONEY
WHERE YOUR
MORALS ARE

PUT YOUR MONEY WHERE YOUR MORALS ARE

A GUIDE TO VALUES-BASED INVESTING

SCOTT FEHRENBACHER

BROADMAN
&HOLMAN
PUBLISHERS

NASHVILLE, TENNESSEE

0-8054-2449-0

Published by Broadman & Holman Publishers,
Nashville, Tennessee

Dewey Decimal Classification: 332.6
Subject Heading: INVESTMENTS
Library of Congress Card Catalog Number: 2001035747

Unless otherwise indicated, all Scripture quotations are taken from the *Holy Bible*, New Living Translation, © 1996, used by permission of Tyndale House Publishers, Inc., Wheaton, Illinois 60189, all rights reserved. Scripture quotations marked NIV are taken from the *Holy Bible*, New International Version, © 1973, 1978, 1984 by International Bible Society.

Library of Congress Cataloging-in-Publication Data
Fehrenbacher, Scott, 1958–
    Put your money where your morals are : a guide to values-based
investing / Scott Fehrenbacher.
            p.   cm.
Includes bibliographical references.
ISBN 0-8054-2449-0 (pb.)
1. Investments—Moral and ethical aspects. I. Title.

HG4515.13 F44   2001
332.6'042—dc21

                                                                    2001035747

        1 2 3 4 5 6 7 8 9 10 05 04 03 02 01

To two godly women who light my path:
my faithful mother and my lovely wife.

"Many women do noble things, but you surpass them all."
PROVERBS 31:29 NIV

CONTENTS

ACKNOWLEDGMENTS

WRITING THIS BOOK has been a great adventure, a labor of love, and would have been impossible without a number of people who were critical in its development.

Most importantly, I wish to thank my lovely wife Joni for her full support and encouragement. Not only did I depend on her through the writing of the book, but more importantly through the path of faith we have walked together in developing the research that underscores this book. Also, I thank my three children—Rainer, Spencer, and Lexington—who have had to sacrifice in many circumstances also.

I am indebted to a number of friends like Jeff Kemp, Mark Davis, Steve Biggerstaff, Candice Atherton McGarvey, and Paul Palmer who counseled me and supported my efforts to write about this subject that God has laid on my heart. Thanks to my mother, my brother Jeff, my in-laws Frank and Darlene Bramon, Joe Forche, Scott Wennermark, and my extended family at Crosswalk.com for lifting my family and me up in prayer over the spiritual warfare that seems to accompany the work of values-based activism.

Gary Terashita of Broadman & Holman is a world-class editor and a man that walks the walk of integrating a Christian worldview into his daily life. It has been a wonderful and inspiring experience working with him. I appreciate his commitment to sharing the foundation of values-based investing that is often misunderstood.

CHAPTER 1

CORPORATE AMERICA AND THE CULTURE WAR

The test of the vitality of a religion is to be seen in its effect upon culture.
ELTON TRUEBLOOD,
The Company of the Committed

"IS THIS WHAT THE END of a civilization looks like?"

Former Secretary of Education and "Drug Czar" William Bennett was reflecting on his thoughts from a meeting he had with Time Warner chairman Gerald Levin in January 1993, challenging Time Warner's choice to exploit music promoting violence, murder, and rape for the sake of profit. Bennett had successfully arranged a private meeting with the chairman at Time Warner's New York headquarters.

He continued to recall the thoughts going through his head while he spoke to Levin at the meeting several years earlier: *You know, this is the end. You are supposed to be leaders. This is Warner Brothers! Is this what happened to Bugs Bunny? Bugs Bunny is now a gangster rapper, talking about how he is going to hurt, mutilate, and torture women?*[1]

Bennett was not the only one outraged at Time Warner's choice to profit at the expense of our culture. Charlton Heston also chose to publicly challenge Time Warner for its decision to sell cultural pollution. In February 1999, Heston had the opportunity to speak to the Harvard Law School Forum about his disgust with corporate leaders' selling out moral values for short-term profits. In his speech, he said,

A few years back I heard about a rapper named Ice-T who was selling a CD called "Cop Killer," celebrating ambushing and murdering police officers. It was being marketed by none other than Time Warner, the biggest entertainment conglomerate in the world. Police across the country were outraged. Rightfully so—at least one had been murdered. But Time Warner was stonewalling because the CD was a cash cow for them, and the media were tiptoeing around it because the rapper was black. I heard Time Warner had a stockholders meeting scheduled in Beverly Hills. I owned some shares at the time, so I decided to attend.

What I did there was against the advice of my family and colleagues. I asked for the floor. To a hushed room of a thousand average American stockholders, I simply read the full lyrics of "Cop Killer"—every vicious, vulgar, instructional word.

"I got my 12 gauge sawed off.
I got my headlights turned off.
I'm about to bust some shots off.
I'm about to dust some cops off. . . ."

It got worse, a lot worse. I won't read the rest of it to you. But trust me, the room was a sea of shocked, frozen, blanched faces. The Time Warner executives squirmed in their chairs and stared at their shoes. They hated me for that. Then I delivered another volley of sick lyrics brimming with racist filth, where Ice-T fantasizes about sodomizing two twelve-year-old nieces of Al and Tipper Gore: "She pushed her butt against my . . . ."

Well, I won't do to you here what I did to them. Let's just say I left the room in echoing silence. When I read the lyrics to the waiting press corps, one of them said, "We can't print that." "I know," I replied, "but Time Warner is selling it."

Two months later, Time Warner terminated Ice-T's contract. I'll never be offered another film by Warner or get a good review from _Time_ magazine. But disobedience means you must be willing to act, not just talk.[2]

While Time Warner has captured more famous detractors than perhaps any other company for its practice of selling violence and profanity, it certainly is not alone.

In fact, corporate America today faces a crisis of bankruptcy. Certainly not in traditional terms of net worth and profitability, but clearly corporate America collectively is facing a crisis of moral bankruptcy greater than at any time in our country's history. I believe it is no coincidence that American companies are increasingly pursuing profitable business ventures without any consideration for the cost the venture will ultimately have on our culture, our families, and our children.

THE BATTLE IS JOINED

Ask ten evangelicals what the culture war is and you will probably get ten different answers. William Bennett often refers to it in his national press interviews as a common degradation of traditional values pervasive throughout our public policies and educational standards. Pat Buchanan describes it as a fight for the soul of America between the righteous and unrighteous. Charles Colson says, "The culture war is not just about abortion, homosexual rights, or the decline of public education . . . . The real war is a cosmic struggle between worldviews—between the Christian worldview and the various secular and spiritual worldviews arrayed against it."[3]

There is no doubt about it. Attempts to destroy parental authority and control in raising children, to dilute our public education system into a godless training ground for social policies while stripping teachers of their authority, to tear down traditional standards in society in the name of fairness and tolerance, and to oversimplify all issues involving violent behavior to a predictable debate over gun control are real encounters in the culture war battlefields every day.

All of these issues, however, leave out perhaps the most powerful and influential battlefield of the culture war. Corporate America as a community has more day-to-day influence on our culture than all of Congress and the executive branch. From the products we purchase to the entertainment we see (with its own brand of morality) to the internal corporate policies that govern our working lives, companies and commerce are at ground zero.

Upon further investigation, there are many good reasons why corporate America represents the most fertile ground for social and cultural change. Corporate leaders have a seemingly straightforward task in leading their respective businesses. That is to seek out a business plan that leads to success as measured in one dimension—profitability. In that traditional measurement, a number of costs are taken into consideration, such as taxes, production, marketing, and labor. Any product that generates higher revenues than costs is generally considered a success.

Yet consider the realm of public policy. When discussing programs, policies, or even products involved with government, the discussion is multidimensional. Not only are the financial costs and profits considered, but the overall value or cost to society is considered. Consider the post-World War II legislation that came to be known as the GI Bill. The result was great initial cost to the government. However, many economists suggested that in the long run these programs would actually provide net income to the government by raising the general level of personal income levels due to a higher average education. This higher income average would lead to higher annual tax collections for the government.

Even more importantly, the discussions considered more than financial costs and revenues. The GI Bill was also endorsed for the positive impact it would have on families, on communities, and on strengthening the country as a whole. Higher education levels would increase the standard of living for all and provide cultural and intellectual benefits for all members of the family.

Politicians and public servants deal every day with the issue of the greater good. They have staffs trained to deal with the public regarding such macro issues—often by having well-trained people giving boilerplate answers to predictable questions. A public official's future often depends on how he or she deals with issues that impact the country and society as a whole.

Unfortunately, this other consideration of value—concerning families, children, and our culture as a whole—is not discussed in today's corporate boardrooms, in product development meetings, or in executive evaluations even though the ultimate influence of corporations on our culture is arguably greater than that of public officials trying to change statutes to the liking of their constituencies. Even with highly publicized events that concern the negative social impact of corporate products, the cultural debate often focuses back on the public policy arena instead of the company or industry responsible for it.

An example: On April 20, 1999, a dramatic tragedy occurred in Littleton, Colorado, that stirred fears of vulnerability among parents across the nation. A collective sense of lost innocence permeated the country after Dylan Klebold and Eric Harris mercilessly murdered thirteen people at Columbine High School and then killed themselves. Parents, pastors, grandparents, children, and students all tried to understand how such an event could take place and, more importantly, how to prevent it in the future.

Only God knows the roots of the behavioral problems that led Klebold and Harris to make their deadly choices that day. Almost immediately after the rampage, the mainstream media served up one more stream of television "experts" and politicians discussing the need for gun control as the ultimate answer. Never mind that there were already many existing gun laws that the two killers broke on that day.

However, more than a day or two later it became clear that both Harris and Klebold had been obsessed with violent video games, such as "Doom," and repeatedly watched *Natural Born Killers* and other movies criticized for glamorizing violence. Harris had also published murderous fantasies related to the video games on his own Internet site.

The connection between the ultraviolent behavior promoted in such video games and the violent behavior displayed by the killers is undeniable. In a May 1999 press conference, even President Bill Clinton said, "We cannot pretend that there is no impact on our culture and our children that is adverse if there is too much violence coming out of what they see and experience."[4] Nearly a year later at congressional hearings, Sabrina Steger also spoke of the impact of violent video games on her life. Her teenage daughter Kayce and two others died in 1997 when fourteen-year-old Michael Carneal opened fire on students holding a hallway prayer meeting at their high school in Paducah, Kentucky.

Steger told the committee, "As a nurse, I'm in the business of recognizing signs of illness, and I see Americans addicted to violence and in denial of it."[5] Steger and the parents of the two other children killed are suing entertainment companies responsible for the violent and sexual video games that influenced Carneal. At the same hearing, Kansas senator Sam Brownback displayed the popular video game "Duke Nukem," which not only was almost exclusively designed around graphic violence and death but also included, as Brownback described, "nude female prostitutes, some bound to posts, begging to be killed."[6]

I applaud Senator Brownback's committee for holding a public discussion on the topic. But I submit that the target of this investigation should include not only public policy but also the source of the products involved. Among all the outrage over the video game "Doom" that the Columbine killers were obsessed with, I have not seen one article, statement, or reference made to the company that chooses to create, package, and sell the product directly to children—a company called id Software.

The company, based near Dallas, Texas, makes other video games such as "Quake" and "Aliens Ate My Babysitter." It was started by friends John Carmack and Adrian Carmack (no relation) in 1990. John, a self-taught programmer, developed the core technology for all of the company's games. The company name was taken from the label given to the instinctual part of the human psyche first identified by Freud.

The company's Web site describes the scenes for the game "Doom" as follows: "You're a space marine armed with a mere pistol. Your mission is to locate more substantial firepower, blow your way through an onslaught of undead marines and mutant demons from hell, and navigate yourself off a radioactive moon base. In order to survive, not only do you have to make it through the first 27 blood-splattered levels of Doom, you also have to get through nine more incredibly tough expert levels in the all-new episode 'Thy Flesh Consumed.'"[7]

The game was first released on December 10, 1993. It quickly attained phenomenal financial success and was recognized as the hottest 3-D action game of all time. Experts recognize it as the catalyst and inspiration for what is now known as 3-D action gaming. In total, an estimated 15 million copies have been downloaded around the world and passed from player to player by floppy disk or online networks. Since its initial product, id Software has also released the sequel "Doom II: Hell on Earth." Doom II has now sold more than 2 million copies. Since "Doom," the company has found even greater success in marketing a more graphically violent series of games under the title "Quake."

An online games expert recently reviewed "Quake": "And forget about leaving the meat behind: Panic Quake is nothing but bodies. Bodies splattered, pulverized and exploded. The body fragged and multiplied, becoming pure speed in a point-to-point network of ammunition flows and tactical lust. All-sucking, all-spewing, the Quakebody is projectile and target, monster and hero, author and interface, key, switch, and trap. It is the body with nothing but organs, irrupting and transmitting, and always forever the barricaded global variable in an infinite cascade of light-speed calculations: surface, perspective, and line of sight—the baroque codes for subjectivity in the digital space of deathmatch culture."[8]

Just as it has become clear to the American public that the companies that produce and market tobacco products have some responsibility for the effects of their products on the health of the public, so, too, should the American public recognize the responsibility companies like id Software have for the effects of their products on the mental health of the children to which they aggressively market. The solution is not to create books full of statutes describing the boundaries of what is acceptable and what is not acceptable—all decided by committee. Rather, the ultimate measurement should be the financial success of the company itself. A company known to be selling poison to people directly will soon be out of business. It will not be able to find investors to back it. It will not be able to find consumers to buy the product. So it should be with a company that blatantly sells products that poison the minds of our children. Let the informed investor and consumer deliver the true accountability.

When we as a society consider the lessons learned from the Columbine High School tragedy, they should involve more than a debate about gun control. Of course the two killers should not have had access to guns. But the source of the behavioral conditioning that led to their choice to use the guns must also be taken into account. No doubt some of this must be on the shoulders of Klebold's and Harris's parents. But there is no doubt that the manufacturers of these same video games must hold accountability as well. As Sabrina Steger told Senator Brownback's Senate committee,

> Violent video games and movies desensitize users to the violence by making it sterile, acceptable, and even desirable. Defilement and carnage all too prevalent on the silver screen is easily transferred to any home by video games seen through hand-held screens, TV screens, and computer monitors.
>
> Blood on the screen has no odor and it cannot be touched. Screams are controlled by the volume button, and slaughter by the on/off button. But the button is too often on, the volume on high, and death repeated each time the restart button is touched. Some question if video games can have that much influence on young people. The entire advertising industry is built on the knowledge that thirty- to sixty-second advertisements influence what soft drink or car we buy and what candidate we vote for. How can we then deny that hours on end of repetitive video game violence does not have a gargantuan impact on impressionable children and adolescents?[9]

Even former First Lady Hillary Rodham Clinton agrees that the manufacturers of these products must be held accountable in the culture war. In a 1993 interview, Mrs. Clinton said, "The lowest-common-denominator quality of much of what appears on television and in other forms of popular culture—the constant barrage of violence and explicit sexuality—reinforces the loosening of human bonds, undermining the evolution of a mature person. For many people, it is affecting not just what they think about but also how they think, because it reinforces a kind of episodic, reactive, almost frantic mode of behavior. I think, on both the actual substance of entertainment and the process by which it's delivered, there are grounds to worry about its impact—particularly on children."[10]

By examining the Columbine tragedy, I believe it becomes clear that a key element has been ignored in much of the dialogue and analysis. There should be more outrage at the products and profits being made by targeting our children with blatantly violent poison that clearly can alter behavior individually, and our culture collectively.

Laws will not stop the id Softwares of the world from targeting children with cultural pollution as long as it remains socially acceptable and financially profitable. When it comes to fighting the culture war, people of faith and all people concerned with protecting the innocence and traditional values for our children must become actively engaged in the battle on the corporate turf where the products are made, supported, and sold with millions of investor dollars. We must engage corporate America where it will make a difference—and that is at the financial bottom line.

Syndicated columnist Cal Thomas said, "Ultimately, there are no permanent solutions to the problems of society in a fallen world. But that does not mean that we should retreat to a monastery and allow social anarchy for the rest of the world."[11] There should be no retreat. When it comes to managing our lives and making decisions, there are consequences that must be considered. We cannot protect our children by locking them in a room. They will interact in a fallen world that, like it or not, we help create and mold by our everyday actions and decisions.

Famed theologian Francis Schaeffer grasped this same belief and argued that for Christians, Christ must be Lord throughout all of a person's life, not through some multiple choice listing as determined by the social standards of the day. Schaeffer wrote, "He is Lord not just in religious things and not just in cultural things . . . but in our intellectual lives, and in business, and in our relation to society, and in our attitude toward the moral breakdown of our culture."[12]

The late Bob Briner left an important legacy that updates and reinforces Schaeffer's message into the new millennium. Briner, cofounder and president of ProServ Television in Dallas and a global pioneer in pro tennis and other sports media, believed that Christians should not only make our relationship with Christ central in our lives, but also give Christ the best we have to offer in life. Briner, an Emmy winner, often referred to modern-day Christians as "lambs" because of our general proclivity to follow and meekly stay out of the affairs of the culture.

He countered that Scripture actually calls for the opposite. As followers of Christ, we owe our best efforts to represent God in all we do. In the entertainment business, Briner observed that most are sinfully content to write for other Christians, sing to other Christians, produce television programs for other Christians, educate other Christians, debate other Christians, and do business only with other Christians. Briner, however, argued against this attitude of separation, believing we must do our best to influence the culture in a positive way by reflecting Christ.

He considered it "shameful" that Christians were acting as lambs while witnessing a culture that needed our message more than ever. He said, "We have failed and are failing America. I am sorry. In failing to show up in the places that really count, where the moral, ethical and spiritual health of our country is concerned, we have left our country exposed and vulnerable to all the ills we now see besetting it. We have not provided a way of escape, even though we profess to know the way."

The solution he recommended was for the lambs to wake up and become "roaring lambs" to engage the culture. Until we start roaring, he said, "Basically, we continue to take the easy way out."[13]

Whether from Francis Schaeffer or Bob Briner, the evidence is unmistakable. The culture war in America today is real. And the battlefields are broader than casting your vote for whomever the latest Christian Coalition survey suggests. If you are serious about your own personal accountability to having Christ as Lord of all of your life, then you must boldly add corporate America and Wall Street to the battle, acknowledging them as potentially the greatest areas of influence in regaining ground for the benefit of your children and our society.

CHAPTER 2

FIGHTING THE BATTLES OF THE CULTURE WAR— AN EXAMINATION

The West . . . has been undergoing an erosion and obscuring of high moral and ethical ideas. The spiritual axis of life has grown dim.
ALEKSANDR
SOLZHENITSYN,
Nobel Prize Winner

AMERICAN HISTORY IS FILLED with chapters of internal dissent over social and cultural issues. Most come and go and are soon forgotten. A few issues, however, develop over time to actually define the soul of the country and its moral direction as a whole.

On March 6, 1857, such an event occurred. On that day, the United States Supreme Court ruled that a slave named Dred Scott could not be entitled to rights as a U.S. citizen and that slaves had "no rights which any white man was bound to respect."[1] Seven justices agreed to deny the personhood of black Americans on that day.

President James Buchanan hoped that the Dred Scott decision would mark the end of widespread antislavery agitation across the country. At first the decision seemed to be a mortal blow to the newly created Republican Party, which was formed to halt the extension of slavery into the Western territories. Of course, the decision proved to be the lightning rod for the antislavery movement that later brought the country to a defining moral crossroads.

13

January 23, 1973, marked a similar watershed event in American history. Once again, the Supreme Court denied personhood—of unborn children this time—when it ruled abortion legal in the *Roe v. Wade* case. Perhaps the Court's 1962 decision banning organized school prayer will be seen in history as another watershed.

Yet when we talk about a culture war in this country, we are talking about more than dissent over unpopular Supreme Court decisions. It is more than protesting a controversial policy at a school board meeting.

Christians nationwide recognized general moral degradation throughout the Vietnam era of the late 1960s and early 1970s and felt powerless to change it. As the anti-establishment voices of the social left pushed free sex and recreational drugs, the differences between a Christian worldview and a developing secular worldview in America were widening and becoming more apparent.

CHRISTIANS IN THE POLITICAL ARENA

In the late '70s a number of Christian activists began to organize movements to respond to this trend. Perhaps the pioneer of this group was Paul Weyrich. Weyrich could not really be labeled a traditional "Christian activist." He grew up Catholic and attended the more strict Eastern Rite Catholic Church, but he believed deeply in the country's conservative values, which he saw eroding away. A former reporter from Wisconsin, Weyrich moved to Washington, D.C., in the late 1960s to be on the staff of a Republican senator from Colorado.

He found financial support in 1974 from the Coors brewing family in Colorado and started his own special interest organization on Capitol Hill—the Committee for the Survival of a Free Congress. Soon afterward, Weyrich was instrumental in organizing other Washington conservative strategists for weekly meetings to discuss influencing the moral compass of the country. The meetings, however—known as the Kingston Group and Library Court—were heavy on substance but light on implementation.

Other groups included the Religious Roundtable, a group founded by Ed McAteer, a former marketing executive with Colgate-Palmolive. His aim was to use the organization to encourage cooperation among various Christian groups nationwide. Also, the group Christian Voice was started by Bob Grant, a former minister. It urged Jews and Catholics as well as fundamentalist and charismatic Christians to overcome their theological differences and work together on political matters.

In 1978, a relatively unknown Baptist preacher from Lynchburg, Virginia, named Jerry Falwell began to deliver the culture-war message directly to the church. Falwell was the pastor of the huge Thomas Road Baptist Church and the leader of its affiliated college—Liberty University. In the summer of 1978, Falwell led his Liberty University singers across the country in rallies known as "I Love America." These rallies were unique in their bold mix of current cultural and political issues with the traditional mission of the church.

Falwell also effectively used the influence of his TV program, "Old-Time Gospel Hour." The program was aired in more than 12 million homes nationwide. With the combined resources of the TV show, his church, and his college, Falwell offered a direct link to grassroots America. And when it comes to politics, an effective voice and delivery system to grassroots America means power.

In May 1979, Falwell invited a group of conservative strategists to a meeting at his Lynchburg offices. The group included Paul Weyrich. The plan was to continue organizing Christians nationwide to influence the political arena for the sake of traditional morals and values. After a lunch break at the meeting, Weyrich told Falwell in private that he was convinced that there was a "moral majority" in the nation waiting to be rallied to action.[2] Falwell agreed, and Weyrich's words were adopted the next month as the Moral Majority was officially founded and announced.

The next year, Christian activist Pat Robertson added the resources of his televangelism show, "The 700 Club," to the political arena as well. He used the program to organize an event called "Washington for Jesus," with the goal of bringing five hundred thousand evangelical Christians to march on the mall in Washington to call for moral renewal in America. The event took place on April 29, 1980, and did attract a half million people. Robertson followed up on the march's success by founding the Freedom Council. This was the beginning of his vision to mobilize millions of Christians in the political arena rather than them being onlookers from the sidelines.

Through many different organizations and by using the untapped power of religious television and radio programming, Christians around the country were invited to influence their society through politics. It was new for most. After years of helplessly watching the moral decline of the country, these organizations promised hope in a new and exciting way.

Perhaps the zenith of this young and growing movement was the election of President Ronald Reagan in November 1980. Amazingly, the mainstream media gave tremendous credit to the Christian voters for Reagan's victory. (Since the 1980 election, the political landscape has associated the Republican Party as the home for Christian and pro-family voters.) Hopes for cultural renewal seemed to be within grasp. Along with the media giving Christians credit for the victory came the immediate perception of political power. Instead of hopes fulfilled, however, the following years generally proved disappointing to idealistic and naive Christians who had no practical understanding of the real world of politics.

Christians new to the process did not understand that Reagan and the Republican Party would not, and could not, simply execute policy changes that would outlaw abortion and pornography and bring prayer back to public schools. The art of politics involves short-term compromise to achieve long-term change. But Christians hungry for influence in our culture did not stand on principles that could be compromised. The cultural issues of the day had the Bible as their foundation.

The decade of the '80s went swiftly downhill for Christian political activists. Jerry Falwell soon was caught up in the financial meltdown of Jim Bakker's PTL scandal. After Bakker's resignation and collapse, Jimmy Swaggart was caught up in his own sex scandal. The fallout was a fatal blow to the political clout and power that the electronic church once represented to the political elite. By the end of the decade, Christians as a voting bloc were being taken for granted by the Republican Party and disrespected by the press.

The Moral Majority officially closed its doors in June 1989. Three months later, Pat Robertson tried to reassert Christian influence in the political arena with the formation of the Christian Coalition,[3] which expanded its agenda from cultural issues to other topics, such as family leave and tax policies. Over time, the coalition did actually prove to be an effective force on Capitol Hill in influencing individual legislative votes. However, its effectiveness was not measured by voting records in Washington, D.C.

By 1996, the weakness of the Christian community in politics was evident. Bob Dole won the Republican Party nomination to run against Bill Clinton for president of the United States. Prior to the convention, Christian activists had been very successful at getting Christians elected to the convention's platform committee. Their responsibility was to craft a broad platform on issues for the party to run on in the coming election year. The platform committee passed a noncompromising pro-life platform consistent with earlier election years.

Dole strategists, however, believed that he had to move toward the political center in order to beat Clinton. When questioned about his commitment to the party's platform, Dole alienated Christians around the nation when he said, "I will not be bound by the platform that's been written and, indeed, I haven't even read it."[4] It was an incredible insult to one of his largest voting blocs.

This demoralized Christian leaders who had felt that the way to win the game was to play by the rules. The rules stated that the platform committee created the political views of the party. But the folly was obvious when the party's nominee flatly said that he didn't really care.

To Christian political activists, the only thing worse than Bill Clinton being elected in 1992 was his re-election in 1996 after what appeared to be his certain political death due to the 1994 Democratic loss of the House and Senate. Clinton's cultural record continued to demoralize Christians. In two short years, Clinton had completely overturned any political muscle that Christians felt they gained through the overwhelming congressional victories in 1994. Four more years of Clinton and Al Gore seemed nearly unbearable, and the mainstream Republican Party was turning its back on the Christian segment.

As if Christians needed a reminder that the culture was degrading further under Clinton's moral leadership, the Monica Lewinsky scandal broke into the news. For the first eight months of 1998, it seemed that every family was under attack by the news media explaining sordid details of Clinton's sex life. Suddenly the evening news had become even more vulgar and trashy than prime-time television.

Ironically, one of the frontline soldiers the conservative activists depended on most turned out to be a casualty in the culture war against Clinton. Newt Gingrich, the Speaker of the House and the inspirational leader of the 1994 conservative sweep in Congress, was exposed to have had an extramarital affair himself. He resigned in shame. This is the same Newt Gingrich who had led conservative forces to oust Speaker Jim Wright of Texas by uncovering a scandal.

In the battle to stand up to Bill Clinton, Gingrich was the biggest casualty. While Clinton remained in office to finish his term and rebuild his legacy, Gingrich departed, taking with him the innocence of many loyal Christian activists who had believed they could make a difference in politics.

A POLITICAL REPORT CARD

In the political arena, Christian activists have spent millions of dollars and invested millions of man-hours. Promises of hope and change have been made to grassroots believers and volunteers. What has been the result? Do the strategies need refocusing? Are battles being won in the culture war?

Ultimately, the answers must come from each Christian individually. However, a few Christian leaders have publicly given their assessment of the movement thus far.

DR. JAMES DOBSON

One event in 1998, perhaps more than any other, articulated the frustration of the Christian community at the apparent ineffectiveness that years of political activism has had on influencing our culture. The event was an address given by the country's most important leader in the pro-family movement—Dr. James Dobson, head of the powerful Focus on the Family ministry. His radio program reaches nearly 12 million people each week.

Dobson accepted an invitation to speak to the Council for National Policy (CNP), a group of conservatives that meets behind closed doors to discuss political and cultural issues. In his speech, Dobson took the Republican Party to task for its record on various conservative,

Christian issues—abortion, parental consent for abortion, pornography, and homosexuality.

Indeed, there is a sense of betrayal out there for what has occurred since 1994 [when Republicans took control of the House of Representatives and the Senate]. I want to reflect that to you, looking at the record in regard to the moral issues. I'm not talking about taxes, not talking about the military, not talking about building bridges and roads and all that sort of thing. I'm talking about the moral foundation of the universe. Those principles that we know are right. Now, in 1994, . . . the Republicans primarily ran again on a pro-life platform. That's what the promise was.

What has been the delivery? Last year, the Republican-led Congress, House, and Senate gave $900 million to Planned Parenthood to take that abortion message around the world. And we're supposed to get excited about supporting that? Talk about betrayal. I told you I wasn't going to pull punches. The man who has probably fought more for the things we believe in than anybody in Congress is Jesse Helms, but he bailed on that one. Jesse Helms bailed out on that! Nine hundred million dollars to Planned Parenthood to go to these Catholic countries, these Muslim countries where they don't accept abortion, to begin to propagandize, to begin to work to spread that horrible procedure around the world. Republicans did that. Shame on them for doing so. . . .

Where are the Republican leaders who stand up and say this is outrageous? We will not stand for it. There was not a peep, a protest from a single Republican leader in the House or the Senate. Not one. Not the conservatives that you know and love. None of them had the courage to speak to that. They're so intimidated. They're so pinned down. It was just incredible. Only Bill Bennett did it. Bill Bennett wrote an article in *Weekly Standard* disagreeing with the president on that and gave a very rational argument for it. He was the only one that I saw. Maybe you saw some of them. I waited for it, and I've since had Senator Ashcroft on my program and others, and I said, "Senator, where were you and where was everybody else?" And he said, "I should have spoken."

Why don't they? I don't know. It's a lack of conviction that there is a boss to the universe and that there are moral standards that we are held to, and we need officials that will stand up and represent them.[5]

CAL THOMAS

Cal Thomas is a syndicated journalist whose column is published in more than 475 newspapers. Early on, Thomas was with NBC News, but a phone call from Jerry Falwell in 1979 changed his career. Falwell told Thomas about his new organization and invited him to become its vice president of communications. Thomas says, "I was the new 'star,' the man who had once worked for NBC News. I was bringing credibility to the Moral Majority, and credibility was the currency one needed in order to be taken seriously."[6]

Thomas has written extensively about his thoughts and conclusions after having been involved on the inside with one of the most active Christian political organizations. "Should Christians involve themselves in politics? To paraphrase the President, that depends on what the meaning of *involve* involves. Should we vote after informing ourselves about issues and candidates? Absolutely! The things that are Caesar's are not only our tax dollars, but our citizenship. Laypeople can organize, peacefully demonstrate, boycott, pray for those in authority (that includes Democrats as well as Republicans), participate in pregnancy-help centers, and lobby elected officials. But they should do so without illusions. Real change comes heart by heart, not election by election, because our primary problems are not economic and political but moral and spiritual."[7]

Thomas also has written, "Two decades after conservative Christians charged into the political arena, bringing new voters and millions of dollars with them in hopes of transforming the culture through political power, it must now be acknowledged that we have failed. We failed not because we were wrong about the critique of culture, or because we lacked conviction, or because there were not enough of us, or because too many were lethargic and uncommitted. We failed because we were unable to redirect a nation from the top down. Real change must come from the bottom up or, better yet, from the inside out."[8]

RALPH REED

Certainly Ralph Reed has earned a perspective on the Christian political movement. He was the celebrated and genius political leader behind Pat Robertson's Christian Coalition. In his book *Active Faith,* Reed is very clear about the limitations of the political process alone in changing our culture.

> Unlike some of our predecessors, our deepest hopes
> for restoring and renewing America do not rest solely on
> our political involvement. In fact, though it may come

as a surprise to some, I believe there are strict limitations to what politics can accomplish. In many cases our best agenda may not be a political agenda at all.

That is not a limiting admission but a vital affirmation. It is an affirmation of Christ's pronouncement that "my kingdom is not of this world." Only after we acknowledge how little government and politics can accomplish are we free to roll up our sleeves and enter the fray with a realistic view of what politics can achieve. If people of faith pour all of their dreams for the reform of society into their political activity, they will not only be sorely disappointed but could set their movement back by decades. We must resist the temptation to identify our religious convictions with the platform of a political party or the election-year platitudes of favored politicians. As Alexis de Tocqueville warned, "[I]n forming an alliance with a political power, religion augments its authority over a few and forfeits the hope over all."[9]

A NEW BATTLEFIELD

The Christian community has focused itself intensely on a few strategies when dealing with our culture. Tactics have almost all been directed at the obvious leading edge of the battlefield—public policy, Supreme Court rulings, and legislation. In short, voter- and court-related issues have dominated the tactics of those culture warriors striving to exercise their democratic influence.

As illustrated earlier, the public policy battle—the struggle to exercise influence democratically through the political process—has been generally unsuccessful. Abortion remains legal, easy, and convenient.

Limited legal successes even in extreme areas like partial-birth abortion are often overturned by activist courts. Even statewide referendums banning special rights for gays and lesbians—referendums that were passed by a *majority* vote at the polling booths—are overturned by the courts.

It is important to note that public policy battles have secured some victory. Many issues of the culture war have been effectively introduced into the public debate and consciousness. Today, political candidates cannot run for important elective office without having to address their stands on these issues. Important public discourse in this country cannot ignore issues important to people of faith. This victory alone, however, will not protect our families and children from continued cultural degradation. This victory alone will not fulfill our responsibility to intertwine our culture with the truth of Christ.

Taking the fight of the culture war to the halls of Congress, to local school boards, and to the public policy arena as a whole certainly is a critical part of a winning strategy. But on its own, as we have already seen from the fruits of the last two decades, it is not enough.

The fact of the matter is, the flank in this battle has been virtually unchallenged even though I believe it remains highly vulnerable. The flank is represented by the dependence of economic prosperity to drive the dark side of the culture war. Much of the reason our culture is degrading so rapidly is because there is an unfettered economic and profit motive fueling it. As long as there are immeasurable millions of dollars to be earned by peddling cultural pollution and as long as the process is free of any tangible or intangible cost to the companies selling it, corporate America will continue to forge ahead down a tragic path for families.

There is a precedent for the place people of faith now find themselves in in this economic battle for the culture. The road has already been traveled by a group of people attempting to influence the culture via the power of investments on Wall Street.

Social leftist activists trying to influence the American culture with their own brand of theology have encountered the same kind of experiences that face Christians today. Nearly forty years ago, the Democratic Party occupied the moral high ground in America in many ways. It was the party of civil rights. It spoke of social reform and encouraged governmental assistance for the poor. Republicans at the time focused on the ballooning budget deficit, the growing power of the government, and the worry about turning America into a welfare state.

Then came the Vietnam War, which turned leftists, academics, and the cultural elite against the old Democratic Party. The principled Democratic Party was about to change. The turning point occurred in the summer of 1968, when the Democrats convened for their national convention. It was one of the last classic conventions in which decisions were made behind the scenes in "smoke-filled rooms" with powerful political machines fighting for power.

Social leftists, pacifists, anarchists, black militant activists, feminist activists, anti-war protesters, and general anti-establishment students saw the convention as an opportunity to hijack the party and bring their own personal issues to center stage. This mix of activists tried to take over the convention with mass demonstrations, violence, and riots, all designed to grab the agenda from the party establishment. As a result, party leaders agreed to accept delegates to the convention based on a quota system designed around race, gender, and sexual preference.

Socially liberal activists soon began to understand that the political and public policy arena was only one means for influencing the culture. Environmentalists, feminists, and anti-war activists began to promote a new tool for influencing the culture. The strategy focused on investors in companies the activists considered environmental polluters, anti-women, and pro-war. By pressuring socially left investors to divest from these companies, they could bring more pressure to bear for their agenda.

This tactic, called "socially responsible investing" (SRI), was seen as a way to "invest for good." In 1988 the movement was officially recognized as potent and formidable when the campaign against South Africa's apartheid policies embraced it. Suddenly, giant retirement plans and endowment portfolios from colleges, universities, unions, and churches began to divest from companies that had operations in South Africa. They believed that the government of South Africa would be forced to make a choice: either change its policies or watch all the multinational companies that had operations there depart because of the increasing pressures on them to leave.

In hindsight, it took the socially left cultural activists twenty years to mature from the point of their first political experience to the embrace of Wall Street as a secondary influence on the culture.

The socially conservative version of activist investing, known as values-based investing (VBI), has yet to find its breakthrough event for Christians to recognize its impact, as socially responsible investing experienced with the South Africa divestiture campaign. By contrast, just as socially responsible investing allows investors to avoid companies that pollute the environment, values-based investing allows people of faith to avoid investing in companies that pollute the culture, such as businesses that profit from abortion, pornography, or forms of anti-family entertainment.

Much like values-based investing is today in its early stages of maturation, the modern SRI movement took years to develop. Amy Domini wrote the first definitive book on the movement in 1984. It took six years past that for the birth of the Domini Social 400 Index that Wall Street has since adopted as mainstream. (This is discussed in greater depth in chap. 7.)

There are many impressive signs that Christians are awakening to the importance of incorporating their investments in their activism. Considering the fact that Christians first formally entered the political area in 1980, will the same twenty-year timespan be in effect? For Christian cultural activists, the road map of the social left offers valuable insight. In the culture war within a fallen world, the fight must be extended to multiple fronts. Environmentalists, gay and lesbian activists, and animal rights activists today understand the importance of combining political influence with the financial muscle of activism on Wall Street.

In a startling recognition of this, *Fortune* magazine declared that the future battleground for the gay and lesbian rights movement is the corporate boardroom. The statement was a declaration that there is less resistance and more cultural influence from corporate policy and products than from the legislative forums in the country. I think *Fortune* magazine is right.

Consider the following: It becomes increasingly difficult for non-Christian elected officials to stand up to the gay and lesbian agenda when companies like IBM and Boeing have already capitulated to accept it. If IBM agrees with the agenda, how could it be called extreme, radical, or immoral? Once these major companies embrace the new definition of marriage and family to include homosexuals and begin aggressively teaching those beliefs in corporate diversity training, how extraordinarily difficult will it be to reverse the trend?

Can you understate the power and influence of the pro-homosexual acceptance message from corporate America? Is it chilling to you to consider that this message is given to employees directly from the same source as their paycheck? It is precisely this same corruptible control over the salary and career of an employee that makes sexual harassment such a brutal offense.

The battle plan is already tested by those fighting the culture on behalf of the environment and gay rights. The time is now for

Christians to respond in the culture war. The political arena continues as a formidable stage. But Wall Street is unrepentant and unchecked in its appetite for profits at the expense of our culture. It is time to live the life of Christ with our money and investments, for, as is often the case, Christ has given us the tools we need to use, and we must recognize it.

CHAPTER 3

SILENCE OF THE LAMBS

The principal provider of this junk says there's a market for it. Time Warner says if we didn't provide this someone else would. I'm sure the people who made the ovens for Auschwitz said much the same thing.
GEORGE WILL,
Commentator

THERE HAS BEEN A LOT of lip service by Christians, other people of faith, and social conservatives regarding the degrading nature of our culture. National leaders of ministries, churches, and parachurch organizations, as well as political candidates, have publicly lamented the trends such as increasing violence among our children, the effects of pornography on families, the mainstreaming of homosexuality as common and acceptable, and the continuing number of abortions in America.

When it comes to the culture war, actions are warranted as an outward expression of faith. Is your Christian walk segmented into the times of the week when it conveniently fits? Do your beliefs permeate everyday decisions concerning your life, your business, and your family? Do we as individuals have an obligation as Christians to uplift our culture collectively to reflect Christ, or do we retreat from what is a fallen world?

As mentioned in chapter 1, the late Bob Briner called on Christians to come out of the closet and live their lives pursuing a close walk with

God while also integrating the truth of the Bible into their lives continuously, not just on Sunday mornings. The impact of embracing a daily Christian walk would be equivalent to the "roar" of a lion, he said; yet as we carry out that walk strengthened and sustained by the Lord's grace and love, we will reflect the lambs that Jesus constantly asked us to be. Roaring lambs. I firmly agree with his concept and have tried to incorporate it into my own life.

Theologian Francis Schaeffer reminds us that the Bible does not differentiate between how we use the truth revealed in the Scriptures. What applies to our lives in church also applies to our daily walk in making choices for our families and our businesses. Our individual choices combine to become the choices of the church body as it impacts our world. We have a responsibility to embrace a Christian worldview in our daily lives.

Charles Colson articulates this concisely in his book *How Now Shall We Live?*: "In every action we take, we are doing one of two things: we are either helping to create a hell on earth or helping to bring down a foretaste of heaven. We are either contributing to the broken condition of the world or participating with God in transforming the world to reflect his righteousness. We are either advancing the rule of Satan or establishing the reign of God."[1]

Similarly, columnist Cal Thomas agrees that as Christians we must understand the consequence of our actions and recognize our role in modern society. Thomas writes, "Because the Christian is a citizen of two kingdoms—one earthly, the other heavenly—he has an obligation to both. He cannot divorce himself from either. He is under divine mandate to both. Nevertheless, he realizes that the one is temporary and the other is eternal. Yet that in no way prohibits his involvement in the temporal; in fact, it enhances it. The Christian cannot merely sit by and passively watch society self-destruct. Something within him—namely, the Spirit of God—cries out for truth and justice. Wherever the cry has been articulated into action, truth and justice have prevailed."[2]

Our role as Christians is illustrated with a question in Psalm 11:3: "When the foundations are being destroyed, what can the righteous do?" (NIV). The psalm inherently suggests that the righteous *should* do something! But what can Christians do to engage our everyday faith in the culture war so that we do not contribute "to the broken condition of the world," but rather choose to participate "with God in transforming the world to reflect his righteousness"?

Surely a number of worthy and somewhat effective strategies have been implemented to counteract the common cultural degradation we see today.

Foremost, and most effective of all, is prayer. The power of our collective intercessory prayer must be part and parcel of any choices we make as Christians in fighting the culture war. Without prayer, there is no effective earthly strategy worth advancing.

As already mentioned, over the years, and specifically the past two decades, Christians have engaged their worldview into the secular political arena with mixed results. They also have participated in letter-writing campaigns, demonstrations, marches, rallies, and loosely organized boycotts.

Success has been mixed depending on how you choose to measure it. Clearly Christians have been able to stimulate dialogue and raise the conscience of the nation regarding issues like partial-birth abortion and youth violence. Unfortunately, many of these activities by themselves are ineffective. Others, such as boycotts, are effective only in making Christians feel good rather than in actually making a difference.

Letter-writing campaigns and boycotts by themselves do not answer Psalm 11:3. If we are to represent the depth of our faith through our actions to a fallen world, do we do it through feel-good campaigns that are nearly ineffective? Psalm 11:3 does *not* say, "What shall the right-eous do to feel better about it?"

The Lord Jesus Christ deserves our very best, and what we have done as the body of Christ in engaging the culture war has fallen very short of that. In fact, I submit that our efforts could be compared to David having chosen to fight Goliath only by yelling at him loudly and throwing a fit. He would have gotten the attention of those around him, but that is all. David could have organized a protest rally against Goliath. He could even have tried to convince everyone that because he was so much smaller than Goliath there was really nothing more he could do. After all, Goliath was a giant. David could have screamed, yelled, protested, and then felt very good about himself. Who could blame him for not doing more?

And if Christians are the David of modern-day society, then who really represents the Goliath of our cultural breakdown today? You might assume it is the Democratic Party by listening to some Christian activists. If not the Democrats or Republicans, are the activist associations like the National Abortion Rights Action League and AIDS Coalition to Unleash Power the real Goliaths that we must tackle? Or what about the companies actually creating, distributing, and promoting cultural pollution today, like Walt Disney and Tenet Healthcare?

I suggest that a statement by Cal Thomas should challenge each of us: "So at the outset we must confront the awesome equality of sin and redemption. We are accustomed to sorting our sins. We put them in a comfortable ranking. Pride or avarice—these are the sins of polite company. Prostitution, drug abuse, abortion, and robbery—these are the sins of a lower class. But in God's accounting, this division is false. There is no moral distinction between the sins of the bedroom and the sins of the boardroom: between the crimes of mean streets and the crimes of Wall Street."[3]

I believe that more than any other, Wall Street is indeed the Goliath we face in the culture war. And clearly, the sins of the Wall Street boardrooms are stealth in the eyes of many.

Colonel Oliver North boiled down the answer to this succinctly when I was a guest on his national radio show. He got it. He identified the somewhat invisible Goliath in the culture war to be those in corporate America who choose to profit from the pollution they are poisoning our culture with. He also articulated the weakness of this Goliath accurately by saying, "Hit 'em in the wallet where it hurts, and their hearts are sure to follow."

That's right. Corporate America is driven by very amoral measurements: profit and market value. If there are negative profit and market-value consequences to companies that choose to sell pornography, provide abortion equipment and material, or actively promote anti-family agendas, there will be a chilling drop in those activities in our culture.

As North recognized, the weakness of this Goliath is very clear—the wallet. Corporate leaders are not all that different from political leaders. Both sets of leaders seek to accomplish personal and professional goals. Politicians pursue agendas that will deliver the votes they need to stay in office or to advance to a higher office. Corporate leaders, similarly, pursue agendas that will deliver the profits and market value they need for them to stay in their positions of leadership or to advance to a higher office.

Just as a politician's vulnerability is evident at the voting booth, a corporate leader's vulnerability rests in the stock market. This is the corporate Goliath's point of weakness today, and Christians have yet to understand it and use it in influencing our culture as we have been mandated to do. Fortunately, we do not have to be pioneers or guinea pigs testing a hypothesis for the first time to see if it is true. Others have already proven the effectiveness of using the stock market to influence corporate America.

Many of the problems that Christian activists have faced can be seen as growing pains. Perhaps these problems are also symptoms of too many Christians not living the Christian worldview in their daily choices, in their daily actions, and in their daily conversations. Just how far are people willing to take the "Christian thing" seriously in their lives?

I believe it is time for Christians with investment responsibility to seek bold solutions to using the power of the assets they control to positively engage our culture. With the collective awesome power they have been blessed to hold, they have the potential to be roaring lambs on Wall Street and within our culture.

For the most part the lambs have been silent. Their power has been caged. My prayer is that the Christian investment community will embrace the call to be salt and light to our world through the influence it holds.

CHAPTER 4

CAPITAL—THE LIFEBLOOD OF CORPORATE AMERICA

Lottery—
A tax on people
who are bad
at math.
A BUMPER STICKER

I LIKE THIS BUMPER STICKER. The reason it is funny is because there is a measure of truth in its humor. Unfortunately, far too many people still believe that Wall Street, the business of personal investing, and the stewardship of personal assets are very much like gambling and the lottery.

It is precisely this misunderstanding that robs Christians and other people of faith of the opportunity to use their money to positively influence the culture for their families and children. If Christ truly is the Lord of your life, then Christ is also the Lord of your personal business affairs. A lack of understanding about how today's corporate capital markets operate simply means you are limited in how you can serve Christ and your family with your money.

As with many other commodities in our society, skilled marketers have boiled down the entire process of investing to its most over-simplified form that can fit in thirty-second commercials and slick newspaper and magazine ads. People used to invest in stocks because they knew what they were buying and felt comfortable with the products. Perhaps it was stock in the company they worked for. Maybe it was the stock of a company that made a product they were impressed with, and they invested to participate in the company's potential profits. Today's financial service advertising sells potential investors convenience and rate of return. Never mind what they own or what that really means. Who has time to know such things?

Yet over the past twenty years, an amazing transformation has taken place—that of bringing Main Street side by side with Wall Street. It used to be difficult and expensive to invest in the stock market and participate in the American dream with the country's prestigious companies. After this transformation—known as the democratization of the markets—access today is as close as your telephone or computer, and individuals are trading at costs that only institutions could get years ago.

In its simplest form, Wall Street is your door to the best of American capitalism. Think about how many times you have mentioned to your spouse or a friend how you wished you owned a certain company because it obviously was "making money hand over fist." Great products, great locations, and great ideas can make money quickly.

Through the stock market, average individuals can easily and economically become part owners of America's best and brightest companies by simply buying shares of their stock. For example, I remember when the first Costco (now PriceCostco) opened in the city where I lived. The large discount shopping club was unlike anything I had ever seen. You could buy a wide range of items, from high-end TV satellite dishes to laundry detergent. In addition, Costco buyers had negotiated with suppliers to create larger quantity packaging than was available to regular grocery stores. With the larger quantities, the discounted price made it even more attractive to consumers.

When my wife, Joni, and I went to Costco, we also noticed the perpetually long lines. It seemed that everyone we knew was shopping there and telling us how much they liked it. We also commented to each other that no matter what we originally came in to buy, somehow we never got out of the store without spending at least one hundred dollars. Yet despite the lines and the high average amount spent, everyone still loved it. I remember telling Joni that whoever owned Costco was surely set up to do well.

Of course, the point is that you and I can own Costco because Costco is a publicly-owned company. That simply means that shares of its stock (part of its ownership) are available to be purchased by anyone through the stock market on a price-per-share basis. You may not be able to buy as much stock as the original owner, but the value of your stock goes up or down the very same percentage as his or hers. You participate equally in the success or failure of that business.

This explanation may well be redundant to you, but many investors with hundreds of thousands of dollars invested in the stock market today do not understand what it really means to be invested in the stock market.

Recently a whole new wave of companies have emerged on the stock market scene to be publicly traded companies in large part due to the "dot.com" Internet stock craze. In the operation of any company, the leaders (the board of directors) have the option of spreading the ownership among just a few or allowing the public to own a portion of the company. They do this by authorizing a specific percentage of the ownership to be purchased by outside individuals through the stock market on a per-share basis.

Of course, among the chief motivations for a company to give up some of its ownership to others through a process called an initial public offering (IPO) is money. The company receives the cash earned from all the initial shares sold on the offering (minus the investment banking fee). In most cases this is preferable to keeping 100 percent of the ownership and borrowing the same amount of money from a bank or going into debt through a bond offering because in both cases that money must be paid back to the people who lent it to you, with interest.

By offering stock to the public, the business of the company is financed, or capitalized, by the investors buying the stock of the company. What's in it for the investor? The investors are hoping that the value of the stock, as measured in a price per share, will be higher in the future than it is at the initial offering. In the simplest terms, the stock price will rise if the future earnings, profits, and value of the company are higher in the future as well.

However, your purchase of common stock is not a lending relationship with the company. You actually *give* the company your money in exchange for a piece of the ownership. You literally become an owner of the company, albeit usually an owner of a very small piece of the company. There is absolutely no promise or implication of a promise to return your money to you. There is only a good faith promise by the company and its board of directors to do everything possible to succeed in the business in which they are involved. If the company is financially successful, the value of your stock should increase, and you will personally profit on the eventual sale of the stock by selling it for more than you paid for it.

One of the most dramatic steps that brought Main Street closer to Wall Street was the increasing popularity of the mutual fund. In America today, most people own stock in companies through a mutual fund rather than through direct purchase of the stock itself. A mutual fund is nothing more than a collective pool of money from thousands of individuals all with the same goals in common. With the one large collective pool, or mutual fund, a professional investment manager is hired in exchange for charging a low annual fee based as a small percentage of the money in the mutual fund as a whole. The investment manager buys and sells stocks (some mutual funds can also invest in bonds or other securities besides stocks) on behalf of the individuals who have put up the money for the fund.

The fund manager's only incentive is to strive for high investment performance. While a traditional stockbroker is compensated by a commission every time he or she helps you trade a stock, the mutual fund manager makes trades inside the fund (which do not cost you any direct commission anyway) only when it stands to benefit your investment performance. This makes mutual funds among the most economical investments in the stock market. (Caution: Not all mutual funds have the same expenses, but many resources are available to help you find lower expense funds.)

With the increasing popularity and access to mutual funds, it became easier and safer for people with less money to invest in the stock market. For example, if you had five thousand dollars to invest in the stock market, you could afford to probably buy into only one or two different companies directly. This would increase your risk by having "all of your eggs in one basket." However, by putting the same five thousand dollars into a diversified mutual fund, your money would be in a pool that overall might own up to one hundred different companies. You would own a piece of each one. Your risk is reduced because if one company has a catastrophic failure, you would not be harmed by being overexposed to it in your portfolio.

Increased activity in the stock market also occurred when company and public retirement accounts began to aggressively market retirement programs like 401(k) plans. These programs allow you to automatically invest a portion of your paycheck, before taxes are withheld, into one or a number of mutual funds of your choice. In fact, this single opportunity was responsible for bringing more individuals into the stock market for the first time than any other event of the last century.

As Americans became more active in investing in mutual funds, the stock market grew to new heights, and a new industry of business news and media was born to meet the demand of investors who wanted to keep track of their money in the markets. Soon companies were started that analyzed mutual funds exclusively instead of the companies that the mutual funds invested in. The funds created their own rate of return, their own histories, and their own personalities even though any stock mutual fund is nothing more than the collection of stocks that it has in its portfolio at any one time. In fact, a few companies even started what are called "funds of funds." These strange investments are mutual funds that use their collective pools of money to simply buy a number of other mutual funds. This separates investors from their ultimate investment by two full levels.

There is no doubt that mutual funds (and other packaged financial products that are very similar, like unit investment trusts) are responsible for new wealth created for millions of Americans. Similarly, they also helped corporate America capture dollars—formerly sitting in bank savings accounts—to finance new growth and new business. It is a classic American economic success story.

Just as with other success stories, however, this new trend has some disadvantages as well. When an investor purchased shares of stock in a company years ago, he received a stock certificate in the mail, acknowledging his ownership in the company. Dividend checks were sent in the mail directly to the stockholder each quarter. What's more, every public company had to invite its shareholders to an annual shareholder meeting at which the board and the officers of the company would be present and accountable for the actions of the company. In fact, the shareholder was ultimately accountable for voting for a board of directors to successfully manage the company. The companies actually involved the shareholders as owners.

Since most people who own stock today own them through mutual funds, they miss out. Mutual fund owners do not get stock certificates of the stock held in their mutual fund portfolios. They do not get their dividend checks because the mutual fund manager either reinvests them back into the fund portfolio or sends them out once a year as annual distributions. Mutual fund owners are not invited to the shareholder meetings of the companies they own. The mutual fund company retains the right to vote collectively on behalf of all of the shareholders represented in the fund, and, yes, this gives these funds a great deal of power. In fact, it is almost universally true that a mutual fund investor has no idea what actual companies he or she owns at any one time.

As you can see, one of the unintended results of the mutual fund industry is to actually shelter the ultimate beneficiaries of the investor's money (that is to say, the companies whose stock is purchased) from the source of the investment money (the investor).

I call it "TV dinner investing." Like TV dinners, mutual funds are packaged for you, include a mix of ingredients, are convenient, and are designed to satisfy your hunger without hassle. Don't get me wrong. I think mutual funds are a terrific tool, but there is no doubt that they have changed the landscape of personal investing. This TV-dinner-investing phenomenon has created a new landscape with clear cultural implications:

First, Wall Street needs Main Street. It is still OK in the culture of Wall Street for the investment elite to snub their noses at the common investor. (In fact, built into the Wall Street culture is something known as the "common man rule." This postulate says that when the common investor on the street begins buying a stock, it's time for the "astute" investors to get out because such a trend is surely a precursor of the stock price going down.) However, as the markets have reached out and attracted billions of dollars of investment money from these Main Street common people, companies now are completely dependent on them in order to keep up their profits and maintain their businesses. This dependency will be discussed in greater detail later in the book because it is this very dependency that makes American corporations vulnerable and empowers the individual investor to use the influence of his money to serve Christ.

Second, truth is separated from consequences. I have already demonstrated why a mutual fund investor loses complete control over knowing what it is he is actually investing his money in. Since the mutual fund manager chooses the stocks that the investor's dollars will buy, the actual investor has no control, and the companies who receive the support of the stock purchase have no accountability deeper than rate of return. In effect, the mutual fund buyer inherently is buying only rate of return because that is traditionally the only aspect for which the investor can hold the fund accountable.

It is important to understand the differences between this and a more traditional investment approach. Allow me to expand by using a hypothetical example.

Assume your neighbor was wealthy and appeared to operate a very successful business. Further imagine that your neighbor approached you with the following offer: "I've been meaning to ask you something. You can probably tell that my company is doing very well. I can't open stores fast enough. In fact, we need to expand to six more cities in the West in the next year. My clients are spending double at my stores than they were this time last year. But I'm looking for a few key people to help finance my expansion. My investors last year have already doubled their money. Look, I wanted to do you a favor and offer you a chance to get in on this. Do you have ten thousand dollars you'd like to invest in my company?"

Of course, the offer sounds interesting, and I think a very high percentage of people would be interested enough to at least ask one follow-up question: "Tell me about your business. What is it that you do?"

This is a reasonable question for someone who just asked you to invest ten thousand dollars in his company. Even though he may be your neighbor, you still may not know this guy very well. I suspect most people would want to know much more about the business, the owner, and the expansion plans specifically before they even considered writing a check for ten thousand dollars.

What if your neighbor answers your question by saying, "I own and operate the nation's largest chain of gentleman's clubs, otherwise known as nude dancing bars. You wouldn't believe how profitable they are!"

I believe the majority of people hearing this would immediately lose interest in this investment, regardless of how well the business was doing or how much money it was making. They would clearly consider it morally wrong to directly support, and benefit from, an activity that promotes casual sex, exploits women, promotes abusive drug and alcohol use, adds to sexual and pornographic addictions, and leads to the break up of marriages and families. Even if you were just one of the investor owners, it's obvious that you would not be serving Christ, your family, or our society with your financial resources by investing in your neighbor's company. Most likely you would simply say, "No, thank you."

Now, compare this example with a different scenario.

Assume your neighbor was wealthy and appeared to be a very successful financial planner. Further imagine that your neighbor approached you with the following offer: "I've been meaning to ask you something. You can probably tell that my practice is doing very well. I wanted to tell you about a mutual fund I work with that has an awesome manager. I can't keep up with the people who want to get into it. In fact, this mutual fund company is growing so fast that it's opening six new offices in the West next year. The fund's size doubled last year. But I'm looking for a few key people who may still be interested at getting in on this fund while it's at the ground level. My investors who were in the fund last year have already doubled their money. Look, I wanted to do you a favor and offer you a chance to get in on this. Do you have ten thousand dollars you'd like to invest in it?"

Once again, there is no doubt that most people would have their curiosity raised. This time, however, I am certain that any follow-up questions would concern the fund's performance, costs and expenses, and the manager's tenure. I can almost assure you (and you can probably confirm this from your own experience) that you would *not* ask questions about what kinds of businesses the fund actually invests in.

It is precisely this disconnect between investor and the ultimate company that has allowed public companies to have access to billions of dollars of investor money without having any cultural accountability to the source of those funds.

Packaged products like mutual funds take on a life of their own, as if the fund itself is actually making the money as a stand-alone business. In fact, many people still believe that it is the mutual fund making the money rather than the underlying companies that the fund chooses to invest in. The funds virtually launder and wash your money of its final moral consequences since the average investor historically has had no way to track where his investment dollars went.

To be fair, it isn't just mutual funds and other packaged financial products (like variable annuities and unit trusts) that end up hiding the businesses in which you invest. The fact is that after fifteen years of aggressive mergers and acquisitions on Wall Street, it is very difficult to know what kinds of businesses an individual company is involved with. So, in the absence of some homework, even buying individual stocks gives you no guarantee of knowing what you invest in.

For example, if you were to purchase one hundred shares of General Electric corporation (ticker symbol GE), you might expect you are buying a company that is primarily an appliance manufacturer. Without a little homework, you may not know that as an owner of GE, you also are helping capitalize Vince McMahon's new XFL. Yes, it's the same Vince McMahon of World Wrestling Federation fame, made rich and famous for the violent and sex-laden wrestling shows that do well in displaying the worst of humanity. General Electric is involved because GE owns the NBC network, and NBC purchased 50 percent ownership of the XFL to become partners with McMahon and the World Wrestling Federation. McMahon's brand of violence and sex, all in the name of entertainment, fared poorly in its first season. Even saddled with the worst Saturday prime-time ratings in the history of network television, NBC is sticking with the league in hopes that its outrageous sex and violence themes will catch on. McMahon stated at the initial press conference that his league will take viewers "where the NFL is afraid to go."[1] Let's hope the news division at NBC doesn't get any ideas about hooking up with McMahon as well.

The point is that very few investors, even knowledgeable investors, know that General Electric is "in bed with" Vince McMahon and the World Wrestling Federation. In today's world of megacompanies, even a washing machine company can be dirty.

Whether you invest through a mutual fund or an individual company, it is difficult to know what you own and how you are earning your money. As companies like McMahon's World Wrestling Federation and the XFL continue to grow, they are dependent on access to individual investors' money. For example, the WWF raised $170 million from its initial public offering on October 19, 1999, as aided by Merrill Lynch, Bear Stearns, and Credit Suisse First Boston.[2] Yet, as has been demonstrated, this flow of money continues to these companies without any accountability for the impact of their products and policies on our culture as a whole.

CHAPTER 5

WALL STREET LAUNDRY

JONI AND I WERE VISITING New York while I was continuing my early research regarding values-based investing. Even though the warm and sunny afternoon tempted us to spend our time strolling around Manhattan, we were both excited to be able to visit the floor of the New York Stock Exchange (NYSE).

I was fortunate to have arranged for a senior floor trader to host both of us during the afternoon. It was my third time visiting the floor and Joni's first. My purpose was to interview NYSE employees and traders in compiling research for building my case for the values-based investing movement.

Our guide told us that he had once been on the NYSE Board of Governors and had spent more than two decades trading securities as a floor trader, otherwise known as a "specialist." Even though I had been at the exchange before, it was always fun to watch one of the seasoned veterans at their craft.

Once we had an opportunity to speak without interruption, I asked him some pointed questions: "What kind of standards does the New York Stock Exchange require for a company to be listed?"

He answered, "The New York Stock Exchange is the most prestigious securities exchange in the world. Companies that are chosen must earn at least $2.5 million pre-tax for three consecutive years and have net tangible assets of at least $40 million. The NYSE considers each company's application carefully on a case-by-case basis. Other factors, like value of publicly held shares and interest in the company, are also reviewed."

I continued, "That's not what I'm trying to get at. I know there are strict financial guidelines involved, but I'm asking about a different measurement of a company's quality. For example, does the exchange consider just what kind of business the company is involved in and the quality of that business?"

Once again, his answer was quick and enthusiastic: "Of course. I can assure you that the New York Stock Exchange has only the highest of standards in admitting companies to the exchange. It would never accept a company that had less than impeccable integrity and credentials."

By this time, I must admit, I began to feel guilty about how badly I had actually set him up for a fall in my line of questioning. He had talked his way into a corner, and he had obviously not recognized just where I was going with my conversation.

"That is what I would have hoped for with the New York Stock Exchange. However, that's exactly why I can't understand why the NYSE would accept one of the world's most prolific pornographic companies to be listed side by side with blue ribbon giants like General Motors and IBM. So how could a company like Playboy get accepted on the New York Stock Exchange?"

His silence was deafening. His eyes spoke volumes. It was apparent that he was angry for being set up and speechless in trying to find an appropriate response. It seemed like an hour, but after a few seconds of silence, the only answer he could muster was, "You mean Playboy *is* listed on the NYSE?" Not surprisingly, our tour ended soon after that.

This conversation made it obvious to me that the leadership on Wall Street takes no real measurement of any kind regarding the cultural costs or implications of the companies it promotes and indirectly capitalizes. Can there be any redeeming value to assisting a company in creating pornographic films and content? Can Wall Street be proud to have opened the door to millions of dollars of capital for Playboy? Can the cherry-wood walls hide the sleaziness and immorality of the pornographic industry?

Today, the New York Stock Exchange publicly states that it "is committed to educating the public about the world of savings and investment in stocks. Whether it's to save for retirement, to fund a college education, or to supplement your current income, the key to successful investing is to be well-educated so you can make smart choices."[1]

I agree completely. But the definition of being a "well-educated" investor needs to be expanded from the traditional view of the NYSE. To Christians motivated to use their resources in a way that uplifts Christ in their lives, being well educated certainly also must include having a keen understanding of just what kind of business partners they have acquired through their stock portfolios.

The example of Playboy as a company not worthy of Christians' investment dollars is a very obvious one. In fact, it is nearly the only pornographic company that many people realize is both publicly owned and involved in making pornography. Americans recognize Playboy as a producer of pornography.

Would it bother you to be an owner of a company that partners with Playboy in distributing its pornography? A few examples: The Houston-based Internet company Telescan (NASDAQ symbol TSCN) specializes in data retrieval tools. It has developed an impressive customer list that includes American Express, BPI Communications, Citibank, Fidelity Investments, Standard and Poor's, PointCast, and Time Inc. New Media. Unfortunately, Telescan also signed an agreement with Playboy to custom design financial quote tools for its Internet sites playboy.com and playboyinvestor.com.

In announcing the new partnership, David L. Brown, chairman and CEO of Telescan, said, "Playboy has a sophisticated audience that expects a level of market data that few companies can provide. We have built into this section some of the most cutting-edge analytics available today to the savvy market watcher."[2] Should it matter to Telescan, to their shareholders and investors, and to David Brown that its new business partner is responsible for the sale of moral poison? Are we really ready as a culture to accept the idea that steady readers of pornography represent "a sophisticated audience"?

Then there's Telocity (NASDAQ symbol TLCT), a leading provider of residential broadband Internet services nationwide. Telocity is not only working with Playboy; it also invited Playboy's chairwoman, Christie Hefner, to be on its own board of directors. In a press release, Telocity explained its enthusiasm for the new relationship with Playboy: "We are thrilled to have Christie join our board at a time when we're preparing to roll out significant new services that will take our company to its next level of development," said Patti Hart, president and chief executive officer of Telocity. "Christie's breadth of expertise building consumer brands—particularly those employing subscriber-based business models—will prove invaluable, especially in the areas of entertainment and gaming."[3]

Not too many years ago, a public company in America would have been ashamed to announce an alliance with a company like Playboy. Even if it had chosen to create a partnership to capture revenue, the company likely would have tried to keep the deal a secret. Today, companies release the information in press releases and even reach out to invite the poisonous influence of pornography onto their boards of directors!

Apparently these companies do not believe Christians are concerned about integrating a Christian worldview into their lives to the point that it influences their investing and consumer decisions. Perhaps in the ultimate measure of disrespect to Christians, corporate America today and the public relations firms that counsel them discount any potential liability to announcing associations with pornographers. Their actions prove that they fear no loss of capital or revenue due to a moral backlash to such an announcement.

Maybe you would be surprised to learn that Playboy is but one example of a public company specifically in the business of creating and distributing hard-core pornography. While it is the most well-known example, many other companies also use money from individual investors to finance their sleaze.

Rick's Cabaret International (NASDAQ symbol RICK), a public company also based in Houston, is self-described as a "premier adult nightclub offering topless entertainment." It was the first of now multiple listings of live adult entertainment companies on the NASDAQ market. Two committees representing NASDAQ actually reviewed the listing application for the company before approving it. When the necessary papers were first submitted for listing on the market, NASDAQ officials stressed that the market, "while not having a morals clause per se, reserved the right to reject offerings that don't inspire public confidence in the market," and Douglas Parillo, an official with NASDAQ, promised that the market would look "very closely" at the proposed offering.[4] Ultimately, the application was approved, and Rick's Cabaret continues as a member in good standing. If accepting Rick's on the market doesn't degrade public confidence in the market, what would?

New Frontier Media (NASDAQ symbol NOOF) is a public company that operates five "adult entertainment networks" for broadcast directly into residences. The networks include Extasy, GonzoX, the Erotic Network, and Pleasure. According to one analyst report, New Frontier Media "features the raciest material that can be broadcast legally."[5] In addition, Private Media Group (NASDAQ symbol PRVT) publishes traditional pornographic magazines (*Triple X* and *Private Sex*) and adult films. There are also pornographic companies that are publicly owned, such as BoysToys.com (NASDAQ symbol GRLZ), and broadcast live nude dancing and sex acts by subscription on the Internet.

Even more disturbing, however, is the fact that many companies' unsavory business practices may be laundered behind the image of a seemingly wholesome brand name. These may surprise you as a potential investor (aka owner) once you look beneath the surface and see what kinds of business products and policies are exposed.

USA NETWORKS (NASDAQ SYMBOL USAI)

USA Networks is a huge entertainment company that operates the Sci-Fi Channel and owns the Home Shopping Network, the USA cable TV channel, and Ticketmaster. The company is also 45 percent owned by Seagrams. Its sales for 1999 were more than $3.2 billion.[6] What you won't find, looking at analyst reports and company descriptions of USA Networks, is the fact that the network has been responsible for developing the ultra-violent and sexually erotic wrestling genre popular on television today. USA Networks partnered with Vince McMahon and the World Wrestling Federation (NASDAQ symbol WWFE) to create a series of wrestling shows shown each week on the network with such titles as "Raw Is War," "Sunday Night Heat," and "Livewire."

To understand just how popular these shows have become, number nineteen out of the top twenty rated shows on all of cable television for the first three-month period of the year 2000 was Monday night WWF wrestling on the USA Network![7] According to the Nielsen ratings, wrestling topped all other cable TV programming. Extreme violence, overt sexual eroticism, and vulgarities are common on these shows. Gone are the days of innocent scripted "good guys versus bad guys" wrestling tales. Today's wrestling product on the USA Networks are infomercials of violence, disrespect, vulgarities, and sex without consequences, targeted to children in our country.

AMERICAN EXPRESS (NYSE SYMBOL AXP)

The financial services, credit card, and travel giant American Express may surprise you when you take a closer look at its agenda. Some companies may support special interest agendas occasionally for public relations opportunities or business partnerships, but American Express is one of the unique companies that uses its policies and the money of its shareholders to specifically promote the homosexual agenda.

American Express has gone far beyond issuing company statements of nondiscrimination against employees and people regarding their sexual preference. It has crossed the line from nondiscrimination issues to actually using shareholder money to advance a social and cultural agenda. American Express recognizes GLOBE—the Gay, Lesbian, Transgendered and Bisexual Employees Association—by subsidizing their organization and its activities with company money, by promoting the organization with internal corporate communications, and by allowing the organization to meet in American Express facilities. Also the company offers domestic partner benefits for same-sex partners of employees. In addition, the company offers homeowners insurance discounts to same-sex couples just as it does to heterosexual couples.

The Gay Financial Network ranks American Express the twentieth top pro-gay and lesbian company in America. The network analyzed companies "in terms of revenues, growth, economic power, as well as how they ranked on issues of corporate policies relating to diversity training, employee benefits, employee groups, nondiscrimination on the basis of sexual orientation in the sale or purchase of goods and services, advertising to the gay market and having in place a ban on any negative stereotypes based on sexual orientation, among others."[8]

American Express has also become a recognized leader in targeting homosexuals in its advertising. Ad dollars targeted to homosexuals have more than doubled from 1994 to the year 2000 when it totaled more than $120 million per year.[9] American Express often advertises in homosexual magazines, such as *The Advocate,* with ads specifically designed for that market.

For example, American Express Financial Services ran an ad that showed two women embracing on a cruise ship, with copy that discussed how American Express Financial Services could meet the unique needs of gay and lesbian couples. In addition, one early American Express traveler's check ad highlighted a new product that did not require the signature of both spouses for convenience. Inset in the ad was a small copy of the new traveler's check. A very close examination of the check showed that the two "spouses" signing the sample check were both women—a fact not lost on gays and lesbians whose consumer loyalty the company was seeking.

TENET HEALTHCARE (NYSE SYMBOL THC)

Tenet is the second-largest chain of hospital facilities in the nation. It manages more than twenty-seven thousand hospital beds with a wide array of medical services, including specialty hospitals, outpatient surgery centers, home health agencies, rehabilitation hospitals, psychiatric hospitals, and long-term care facilities. Unfortunately, Tenet Healthcare also manages some hospital properties that perform for-profit elective abortion services. Shareholders, or owners, of Tenet Healthcare can find themselves as unwitting recipients of money paid for taking the life of unborn children.

J. P. MORGAN & CO. (NYSE SYMBOL JPM)

One of the oldest and most prestigious financial firms on Wall Street, J. P. Morgan & Company is often mentioned as the standard for pedigree and integrity in the financial services industry. The same company also has the reputation for being one of the most steadfast financial supporters of Planned Parenthood. The company has spoken on behalf of its shareholders by sending hundreds of thousands of its shareholders' dollars to support the leading pro-abortion group in America—Planned Parenthood.[10]

WALT DISNEY & COMPANY (NYSE SYMBOL DIS)

The same company that made films like *Cinderella*, *The Absent-Minded Professor*, and *20,000 Leagues under the Sea* has paradoxically turned into one of the leading anti-family entertainment giants in the country. Disney is the third-largest media conglomerate in the world.[11] Among its subsidiaries are the ABC television network; the ESPN and A&E cable networks; the film studios Touchstone, Hollywood Pictures, and Miramax; and the famous Disney theme parks.

Of all of the companies that I mention when I speak to groups or on talk radio shows, Disney seems to get the greatest attention. Even though there has been an active boycott of Disney products for a few years, organized by a coalition of denominations and ministries, the public still expresses shock at the extent to which Disney has chosen to degrade itself.

The shift at Disney began when the company seemed unable to find a formula for making profitable films in the early 1980s. In an attempt to rescue the company from its slide, Disney hired former Paramount Pictures president Michael Eisner on September 22, 1984.[12] After attracting many loyal and former Paramount executives, Eisner began to expand the audience for Disney films by adding adult-themed movies to its traditional family themes. To find a studio that could create these films but not specifically have the Disney name, Eisner offered Bob and Harvey Weinstein a buyout of their Miramax film studio in September 1984. The Weinsteins were nearly $12 million in debt to Chase Manhattan Bank at the time. They had produced such films at Miramax as *Tie Me Up, Tie Me Down,* which was given an X rating, and *The Cook, the Thief, His Wife, and Her Lover,* which included a brutal sex scene, mutilation, and graphic violence.

Disney's new subsidiary, Miramax has since created a number of films that glorify violence, drug use, promiscuous heterosexual and homosexual sex, random murder, and rape while simultaneously mocking people of faith. Its portfolio of films under Disney includes the graphically violent and vulgar *Pulp Fiction,* the blasphemous anti-Catholic film *Priest,* the *Scream* series of horror movies, and others such as *Trainspotting,* a movie about a group of HIV-positive heroin addicts.

Priest, which Disney released in April 1995, is fundamentally anti-Christian and anti-Catholic. The movie features a character who is both a Catholic priest and gay. He cruises gay bars in search of his next sexual fling. The character is sexually aroused by the crucified body of Christ ("a naked man hanging there writhing in pain, utterly desirable!"). The character is implied to actually be more moral than his counterpart—a conservative priest who is secretly sleeping with his housekeeper in an illicit heterosexual affair. In total, the movie contained four scenes in which a priest was engaged in graphic sexual acts.

In 1994, a Disney subsidiary released the film *Kids,* which *Variety* magazine called "one of the most controversial American movies ever made." The movie was disguised as an artful commentary on the pressures facing urban youth while glorifying free sex, vulgarities, and drug abuse among preteens. *Newsweek* magazine said, "The film follows a number of barely pubescent-looking boys and girls around New York City as they smoke pot, bait gays, beat a black man, and engage in graphic sex." This movie clearly crossed the line of soft porn more commonly found in movie theaters and instead qualified as pure pornography.

In their book *Disney, the Mouse Betrayed,* Peter and Rochelle Schweizer offer their insights into the movie *Kids:*

> The most disturbing thing about the film are the lurid sexual images of children, images that Professor Richard Mohr at the University of Illinois calls pedophilia. . . . Mohr has written several books on sexuality and essays like "Knights, Young Men, Boys." He has also been active in the gay marriage movement and writes frequently about doing away with "traditional notions of marriage and sexuality." But when it comes to *Kids,* Mohr notes that "Clark [the director] has carefully larded his film with kids' naughty doings in order to distract the critics' view from the cinematographic point of the movie which is to linger on naked boys—naked boys shooting the macho breeze." He correctly notes that the film's pseudodocumentary style is simply a vehicle to obscure the theme. "The documentary style makes the pretense of simply 'presenting the facts'—a would-be charitable and disinterested act," he writes. "But this posturing simply serves to insulate both the director and viewer from taking responsibility for the movie's voyeurism, its visual lusting for kids."[13]

Beyond making anti-family films, disguised under non-Disney studio names, the company has also actively pursued a pro-homosexual agenda. In addition to providing domestic partner benefits to same-sex partners of employees, Disney also has created one of the most active and well-known gay and lesbian employee organizations in corporate America. The group is Lesbian and Gay United Employees (L.E.A.G.U.E.).

The company has earned many awards from within the homosexual community for its pro-gay policies. The Gay Financial Network has named Disney the fourteenth "most powerful gay-friendly public company in corporate America" for 1999.[14] In the 1994 book *The Ten Best Companies for Gays and Lesbians,* author Ed Micken chose Disney as one of his top ten companies to highlight.[15] In addition, the company has financially supported a number of homosexual causes. For example, Disney was a corporate financial supporter for the 2000 GLAAD (Gay and Lesbian Alliance Against Defamation) Media Awards.[16]

There are many other public companies whose actual businesses and agendas may surprise you, companies like American Airlines, American Home Products, Abercrombie & Fitch, and Benneton. I reiterate the counsel of the New York Stock Exchange: ". . . the key to successful investing is to be well-educated so you can make smart choices."[17]

Ironically, I recall that years ago one of the largest shareholders of the company that created "Beavis and Butthead" was a mutual fund supported by the American Association of Retired Persons. The irony was great—senior citizens in America had unwittingly invested tens of millions of dollars into MTV and its Beavis and Butthead characters who went so far out of their way to disrespect the culture that many senior citizens worked their whole lives to create.

I am certain that if their money managers had given those senior citizen investors a choice of whether to invest in Beavis and Butthead and MTV, they would have answered with an emphatic *no!*

CHAPTER 6

STREET FIGHT—
ENGAGING WALL STREET
AS A SHAREHOLDER

*The fact that,
compared to the
inhabitants of
Africa and Russia,
we still live well,
cannot ease the
pain of feeling
we no longer
live nobly.*

JOHN UPDIKE,
Novelist

ELIZABETH DOLE DIDN'T just complain about Walt Disney. She wasn't satisfied just listening to the outrage on talk radio and telling her friends about it in church. She wasn't complacent enough to justify inaction by throwing her hands in the air and saying she was powerless to do more. She didn't worry what the theological implications would be of acknowledging her desire to reform part of the secular world.

Elizabeth Dole put her money where her mouth was. She sold her Disney stock. Was Disney abhorrent to her for releasing the movie *Priest*? Yes. Was she outraged at Disney's (through Hollywood Records) recording artists selling racist-themed music? Yes. What did she do? She took action where it mattered most. She discontinued her business partnership with Disney by selling her stock in the company.

Special interest groups have recognized the unique influence and power of the corporate structure for many years. This influence has been used with varying degrees of effectiveness through different kinds

59

of tactics. Known as shareholder activism, groups have changed corporate policies and products through their organized strategies.

Ironically, it was the church that began much of the shareholder activism movement in the 1970s. Specifically, the Catholic Church and more socially liberal churches were active in trying to encourage what they defined as "social justice" through influencing corporations. Their approach was both tenacious and conciliatory. Churches used selective investment screens to avoid "sin" companies involved in the production of tobacco or alcohol products.

The strategy was to target public companies and get a "shareholder resolution" placed on the ballot of the company's annual meeting. Once an item was placed on the agenda, the activists hoped to force a vote by the shareholders of the company on any policy they wanted. Public companies are set up democratically, with each share of common stock traditionally carrying one vote with it. In most cases, however, the activists knew that there was no way they could successfully muster a majority of votes to support their cause. Hoping that the public image might shame a company into changing its internal policies, the activists actually defined success as being able to force a public dialogue on an issue that the company would prefer to keep quiet.

It was in 1970 that the Securities and Exchange Commission, which regulates company-shareholder interaction, agreed to allow political, social, and policy issues to be admissible for consideration at annual public shareholder meetings. Since then, at last count, at least 111 companies have considered at least 157 shareholder resolutions on at least a dozen social issues. Most have been socially liberal issues, such as animal rights, the environment, nuclear exposure, or military and weapons production. In attempting to actually change policies, these shareholder resolutions have been ineffective. Their principal result has been to raise public awareness of the issues concerning a particular company.

This passive strategy has matured to the more effective role of active divestiture. In other words, rather than trying to change a company's policies by targeting the shareholders in a vote, a group tries to make a company capitulate to its demands by targeting those people investing in the company. The theory is that if money is taken out of the company—divested—the company managers risk losing their own jobs due to a drop in the price of the stock. (By selling company stock, the demand for the stock falls and so does the price. This lowers the market value of the company, which is one of the key measures of success for any corporate management team.)

Basically, a successful divestiture campaign forces company management to decide which is more important—continue with the policies and products as status quo and risk losing millions of dollars of market value or give in to the demands and change accordingly to avoid any further loss of market value.

For example, the tobacco industry is now under severe pressure because of the effectiveness of the present divestiture campaign. Already, many medical schools have voted to sell tens of millions of dollars of stock out of their own endowment portfolios in an effort to keep the consciences of investors clean and to punish the tobacco companies. Harvard, Johns Hopkins, Wayne State University, and the City University of New York are but a few that have sold their tobacco holdings.[1]

In addition, a state of Massachusetts tobacco divestment measure ended up selling more than $230 million of tobacco company stock from state-owned portfolios. Former Massachusetts governor Paul Cellucci said, "We should not profit from the same people who are encouraging our children to smoke." Other states and universities are following this lead. Loss of market value and market demand for tobacco company stock, combined with litigation threats, continue to put an incredible amount of pressure on these companies.

In another manifestation of the divestiture strategy, huge pension and retirement plans are beginning to flex their vast financial muscle.

For example, the California Public Employees' Retirement System, otherwise known as CalPERS, is one of the largest retirement funds in the country, with more than $150 billion in assets. CalPERS uses both its voting power and the threat to sell assets in trying to influence a company in its stock portfolio.

In 1998, CalPERS owned 569,000 shares of Marriott, which was valued at more than $40 million.[2] CalPERS disagreed with a Marriott proposal regarding new corporate policies and a proposed merger with the France-based Sodexho Alliance. CalPERS's efforts found success in changing the proposal.

In addition, the Disney Company faced a similar threat from another megaretirement plan: the College Retirement Equities Fund. The fund, or CREF, has more than $250 billion in assets and is the largest retirement fund in the world. CREF has been particularly active and effective in its shareholder activism. In 1998, CREF urged Disney to increase the independence of its board of directors and to reduce the huge executive salaries that it was granting.

CREF at the time owned nearly 6.9 million shares or about 1 percent of the outstanding shares of Disney, valued at $700 million. In the CREF complaint, its statement said, "An overwhelming majority of Disney directors are closely affiliated with either the company or its chief executive, Michael Eisner. It also questioned compensation packages awarded to Eisner and other Disney executives, including former number-two man Michael Ovitz."[3]

CREF has been extremely effective in exercising its influence of shareholder activism with the threat of divestiture to get what it wants. For example, in the first five months of 2000, CREF urged ten public companies to increase the independence of their boards, and six immediately complied. In addition, CREF urged seventeen companies represented in its portfolio to remove "poison pill" anti-takeover measures that might have reduced ultimate shareholder value. Within a few months, fifteen of the companies agreed with the demand.[4]

You might sense that these large retirement funds are acting as bullies to force their own agendas down the throats of the companies in which they own stock. If that is the case, I ask you to reconsider your feelings. Remember that retirement plans own large portions of companies. They are exercising their responsibility to oversee the management of the companies in which they own shares. Leaders of publicly owned companies are well aware that owners have influence with the company if enough shareholders can effectively organize into a common voice. This is the way public ownership was designed in the first place. These are the checks and balances of the public company so often overlooked by individual investors.

This system of checks and balances is designed to protect investors from company management that may fail in increasing value to the company. If a company loses the faith of the investors, then the stock price will fall as many sell their holdings. The board of directors responsible for the health of the company may lose faith in the ability of the management team, the officers of the company, and subsequently move to replace them. The board would hope to restore faith with a new management team, according to the wishes of the investors in order to invite them to buy in again and regain the market value that had been lost.

It is clear how Christians and people of faith can utilize these common policies to exercise a responsible influence on specific publicly owned companies as we take on the Goliath of our culture war. The blueprint is prepared and has been proven to work effectively.

What, then, is the responsibility of the Christian shareholder? Has it been demonstrated that the Scriptures clearly indicate that Christ should permeate our business lives as well as our personal lives? I believe it has. Has it been demonstrated that Christians have a moral obligation to extend their worldview to the development of the culture around us, even though it is in a fallen world? Yes, I believe it has. Has it also been proven that Christians, like any other special interest group, have the ability to influence Goliath-sized corporations? Yes, there is no doubt that it has.

Consumer boycotts are OK. Letter-writing campaigns to politicians help us feel better but accomplish little else. Rallies are important to raise public dialogue. But I believe that Christ expects us to attack Goliath directly and to exercise our faith boldly in the face of anti-family companies whose practices are antithetical to a Christian worldview.

This is one thing that the righteous should do in answering Psalm 11:3. Christians as individuals may have one of the greatest tools of influence in our culture and not even recognize it. It is our own money—the money invested in personal accounts and retirement plans. With each share of stock ownership, Christians have a voice that can be exercised. And perhaps the greatest power of your voice is not in owning a company and trying to change it but actually in denying anti-family companies access to your money and divesting your money from them.

Elizabeth Dole was willing to do this. She was outraged by the heretical garbage that Disney was willing to produce. She denied Disney any further access to her own money and found an alternative investment that I am sure has performed just fine.

As individuals, we must answer Psalm 11:3 just as Elizabeth Dole did. The culture war is not someone else's problem. It falls on our shoulders individually. Abortions will not be reduced by simply writing a check to a pro-life association once a year and expecting that organization to do all the work for us.

ASSUMING RESPONSIBILITY FOR CHANGE

Values-based investing is not simply about protesting those invest-ment portfolios that hold dirty companies. It is about a commitment to hold portfolios that not only represent sophisticated tools for high investment rate of return, but that also reaffirm the thousands of companies in America choosing to conduct their business in a culturally clean or neutral fashion. It is about investing in businesses you can believe in financially and morally. It is about seeking out business partners you can be proud of in front of your family, in front of your pastor, and in front of the Lord.

In my years of promoting the methodology and philosophy of values-based investing, I have come across a number of opportunities to explain the scriptural basis and virtues of it. I find that Christian money managers are almost universally surprised to find out their investments may include holdings in pornography and abortion-profiting businesses.

It is one thing for the managers to continue their work without this data or without knowledge of how to access it. It is quite another burden of responsibility to know that holdings in your portfolio are offensive and then choose to ignore it. I've had hundreds of discussions with financial advisers and money managers, and it is immediately obvious in their eyes when this recognition hits them. With some of them, it is almost as if they wish they could erase this knowledge, turn back time, and continue in blissful ignorance.

At first, many are tempted to hide behind their "inability" to compromise the rate of return of their customers, saying they are "unable" to integrate such screening on their work. But when they see data that conclusively illustrates that there is no reason to accept a lower rate of return (refer to chap. 7), they once again feel a new burden of responsibility. Rightfully so. To an investor and a professional financial adviser who represents Christian investors, this is the moment of truth. We must choose to use the tools God has blessed us with to engage the culture as we have been commissioned to do.

One national ministry stands out in my experience as immediately stepping up to the plate. I was invited to appear on the "Beverly LaHaye Live" national radio show in Washington, D.C. Of course, Beverly LaHaye is the leader of the respected Concerned Women for America (CWA) ministry. Mrs. LaHaye was well prepared and professional in her interview. She was sincere and passionate in her questions.

After the interview I met the chief financial officer of CWA, Lee LaHaye, and explained the philosophy behind values-based investing. Using a Washington-based Christian financial adviser, Lee directed that the retirement funds of CWA be immediately converted to an alternative plan that provided screening coverage. The LaHayes are examples of ministry leaders who take their stewardship responsibilities seriously and act on them immediately. CWA members and financial supporters should be extremely proud of the quick action and choices their leaders made in order to add one more tool to honor the Lord and work toward reducing cultural pollution in our society.

In subsequent radio interviews with Mrs. LaHaye, she has stated that she has instructed her Merrill Lynch broker in her hometown to integrate the screening philosophy into the investment choices that he would offer her. Even though there is no reason to believe she will have to compromise her rate of return, not once did she express a concern to me that she would have to do so.

In another example, the director of investments for a major denomination in the country led an effort to create a receptiveness for values screening in the denomination's investment portfolios. He, like many others, ran into trouble when it came to identifying what is acceptable and what is unacceptable. Specifically, he wrestled with the question of boundaries on screens.

It was obvious that the screens should keep out the Coors Brewing Company, for example. But what about the companies that manufacture ingredients that end up in Coors beer? The investment director's questions also included just how to define a nonmarried lifestyles screen so that his investments could avoid companies with policies that promote heterosexual nonmarried partners living together and likewise avoid companies that promote homosexual partners living together. Kudos to this denomination for taking a leadership role in this area. Since we first met, I have worked with this director to help answer his questions as he works to create a definitive and sound values-based investing policy.

On the other hand, there are many disturbing examples. A 401(k) plan of a national pro-life organization had some fairly significant exposure to companies that produced abortifacient products and to hospital properties that actually profited from performing elective abortions.

There is no doubt that if financial contributors to this organization knew that the leaders did not take measures to keep their money from flowing to the businesses of abortion, many would be outraged. I pray that these leaders will understand and recognize that they have a stewardship responsibility to their contributors and to the Lord to stop capitalizing and profiting from the business of abortion.

It is important to clarify that there cannot be a universal screening methodology that meets the needs of all Christian investors. Through research I have created resources to help individuals test companies and mutual fund portfolios according to the investor's personal screens and tolerance level. The information is designed to allow investors to determine their own needs and screens first and then scrub their portfolios to the tolerance levels they select themselves.

Sadly, I also have discovered some so-called ethical mutual funds that hold hundreds of millions of dollars from Christian individuals, colleges, retirement plans, endowments, and foundations in investments in unethical companies. Here are some examples: Lutheran Brotherhood Fund, MMA Praxis Fund, Domini Social Equity Fund, Catholic Values Investment Trust, and AAL Equity Fund.

It can seem overwhelming to find what appears to be many funds filled with companies profiting at the expense of our culture. Do not despair. The vast majority of mutual funds on the market are clean and free of such offensive holdings.

Jesus was very clear that our role on this earth was to be salt and light. Bob Briner, in his book *Final Roar*, said that being salt and light has nothing to do with talent, ability, or being appropriate for just a special class of believers: "Neither is it an option to be considered. It is a command to be obeyed. It is the responsibility of every Christian to make being salt a regular, systematic, cogent part of our lives as Christians and to be sure that we offer Christian perspectives, Christian alternatives, and biblical answers to those with whom we have regular contact."[5]

Professional financial advisers and money managers who are Christians and who serve a Christian clientele should come to the same conclusion. They already have a responsibility to search for companies that have strong earning potential. Their fiduciary responsibility must also recognize a stewardship responsibility to provide a Christian perspective on potential investments as well as positive alternatives. This recognition of being salt and light through their professions has come very slowly.

I was invited by a worldwide money manager based in Tacoma, Washington, to discuss the work I had done with cultural investment screening. This billion-dollar secular company had created a management committee to spend a year evaluating a program called the Church Market Initiative (CMI). It correctly identified more than a billion dollars presently invested in funds and portfolios collectively by churches or parachurch organizations. The company wisely was seeking an edge with the churches to attract the money into their portfolios in order to earn the lucrative annual management fees measured in millions of dollars.

A committee peppered me with questions about how I developed my methodology. We bantered back and forth on screen definitions. It was clear the committee members were very uncomfortable when it came to discussing a screen for identifying companies that overtly use company money to promote homosexuality. I could tell that they wanted to skip that. After a few hours I could see that the group was frustrated that it couldn't identify "Christian" screens on which everyone could agree.

I later found out that the final conclusion of CMI was that there was no way to establish a common set of screening criteria that satisfied Christians and was still politically correct enough to market. What the committee members didn't understand is that the movement is not a marketing gimmick designed to increase sales; it is the fulfillment of making daily choices that uplift Christ in our lives. It is the fulfillment of our challenge to engage a degrading culture as roaring lambs.

Equally frustrating are the large denominations that have hesitated to take a leadership position in providing screening for their members. Church denominations collectively control hundreds of millions of dollars. Together, denominations could begin to make a difference on Wall Street by denying pornographers and pro-abortion businesses access to their money. Church members should have the peace of mind of knowing that the national denominations they support do take the time to protect their tithes from being invested in cultural polluters.

A Houston-based private money manager called Capstone Financial was bold enough to endorse and support an initiative to create a new index mutual fund called the Christian Stewardship Fund. As an index fund, it would simply track the Standard and Poors 500 stock index as far as performance was concerned. The difference is that the index was scrubbed for companies that failed the cultural screens. The end result was a low-cost index fund designed to deliver the same return as the S&P 500 without any of the offensive companies found in the S&P 500.

In marketing the fund, a company vice president named Don McFadden spent months flying across the country to meet with the treasurers and investment officers of some of the country's largest denominations and ministries. In many cases the treasurers gave verbal encouragement to McFadden to move ahead. In some cases promises were made to support the effort by investing a fraction of the denomination's money in the index fund. Some promises materialized. Others did not.

So far the fund is performing just as was hoped. I would not be surprised if its rate of return outperformed many of the existing investments of the denominations. In the same way, I would be surprised if the management costs of this fund were not lower than the majority of those the denominations had.

When a private company like Capstone decides to risk a good deal of its own capital to support an effort to give Christian money managers an opportunity to invest with their convictions, the body of Christ should go out of its way to support it. When an opportunity comes along to make a choice to impact our culture by doing something positive, we should embrace it. Would it have been more successful to have solicited the denominations for contributions to a campaign to condemn the abortion industry and Hollywood? The way to change our culture is by proactively offering positive choices for Christians to affirm their faith and convictions.

CHAPTER 7

WHY SHOULD WE ACCEPT A LOWER RATE OF RETURN?

"If you are willing and obedient, you will eat the best from the land."
ISAIAH 1:19 NIV

OVER THE PAST FIVE YEARS I have discussed, explained, and encouraged countless Christian leaders about the virtues of considering the moral values of their investment money just as strongly as they consider the rate of return they expect on their investment money. I have also personally discussed this methodology with hundreds of Christian financial advisers and portfolio managers for Christian organizations.

In most cases I have encountered one grave response: "How can you ask me to avoid investing in offensive companies when I may sacrifice my rate of return?" This is a very predictable concern and question. Furthermore, one striking aspect of these responses is the evident fear associated with the prospect of making changes. Clearly, to many folks, letting the "sleeping dog" of investment values lie undisturbed is preferable to facing a moral decision and its consequences when choosing investments.

The irony in this fear is that there is no law, physical or divine, that precludes a values-friendly company from performing just as well financially as a "values-challenged" company. I have always been amused at why so many people automatically assume that those very few companies that fail a values screen must inherently make more money than those that pass.

In fact, I don't remember reading any Scriptures that say (1) "Sinful business practices will be blessed more than those that are not," or (2) "Followers of Christ shall follow the will of the Lord in all aspects of their lives, unless it reduces the rate of return on their portfolios." I've looked, and these verses just aren't in the Bible!

The good news is that, in fact, *there is absolutely no reason to believe* that just because you choose to be obedient in your investment choices you have to accept a lower rate of return. Christians do not have to face a trade-off between morality and rate of return. The evidence and research is quite clear that morally neutral or clean investments and superior rates of return are not mutually exclusive. I would like to analyze the evidence that leads to this conclusion.

CHOICES ARE ABUNDANT

In all of my research reviewing more than ten thousand publicly owned companies in America, the results are fairly consistent that no more than 5 percent of them fail a common set of Christian-based values. The screens applied identify business practices or policies that are harmful to families or degrade the scriptural and traditional definition of the family.

Since less than five hundred of these companies fail such screens, values-conscious Christian investors have nearly ninety-five hundred morally neutral or clean companies from which to choose in assembling a profitable portfolio. This statistic often comes as a surprise to many Christians.

The number of public companies listed on exchanges has grown dramatically over the past twenty years. This is an important development for screened investing, such as values-based investing. As an investment professional assembles a stock portfolio, certain industries will be selected for the portfolio and allocated financially in predetermined percentages. The actual percentage of the overall portfolio that each industry represents is based on the performances each industry is expected to have in the coming year.

For example, an industry formula for a popular mutual fund, the Gabelli Asset Fund,[1] is designed as follows:

Utility companies	3.9%
Energy companies	2.1%
Financial companies	7.2%
Industrial companies	12.2%
Consumer durable companies	5.2%
Consumer staples companies	9.9%
Service companies	50.8%
Retail companies	2.6%
Health companies	2.9%
Technology companies	3.3%

As you can see, the manager of the Gabelli fund has emphasized the area of service companies in the portfolio. This formula reflects his expectations of which industries are going to perform the best over the coming months.

The next step in building the portfolio is determining which stocks within each of the industry classifications are the best to buy. This is done through traditional fundamental and technical research. In other words, an investment manager analyzes variables such as earnings per share, cash flow per share, price to book value, and strength of management. In addition, a manager may consider how the stock's present price compares to its twelve-month high and low as well as the pattern of the stock's price chart for the past twelve months. Many institutional managers now use sophisticated computer models that analyze such financial information for thousands of stocks.

In either case, a list of attractive stocks within each industry category is available for the manager to choose from. For example, the listing for the most attractive companies in the services industry could look like the following:

Company	Symbol
Comcast Corporation	CMCSK
USA Networks	USAI
Paxson Communications Corporation	PAX
Marriott International	MAR
Boston Properties	BXP
ProLogis	PLD
Global Crossing Limited	GBLX
Nippon Telegraph & Telephone	NTT
Sonera Corporation	SNRA
Metromedia Fiber Network	MFNX
VoiceStream Wireless Corporation	VSTR
US West [Quest]	USW
American Tower Corporation	AMT

From this list, the manager could choose those that would ultimately be purchased for the portfolio.

An important factor in screening investment portfolios for social or cultural considerations is abundance of attractive companies available within industry groups. Twenty years ago, fewer public companies were available. Consequently, there were fewer attractive companies within each industry group from which to choose. Of course, adding another "test" for selecting companies potentially eliminated many attractive companies within each industry classification, resulting in a diminished investment rate of return.

However, because there are so many publicly owned companies today available within industries, eliminating companies that fail values-based investment screening does not inherently diminish high-quality choices. This fact is important in recognizing that cultural screening does not lower your potential investment rate of return. In fact, based on the example above, the only companies that fail values-based screens are US West (for promoting nonmarried lifestyles), Marriott (for distribution of pay-per-view hard-core pornography), and USA Networks (for development and distribution of anti-family entertainment). As you can see, there still would be an abundance of attractive companies left for the manager to choose from, even considering the new VBI screens.

ACADEMIC EVIDENCE

There is a great deal of support for the belief that companies that are not family-friendly stand no greater opportunity for investment performance than clean companies. Research into the theory of efficient markets also makes a strong case for the viability of values-based investing when it comes to performance.

A recognized expert on the patterns of modern markets is Professor Burton Malkiel of Princeton University. His famous book, *A Random Walk Down Wall Street,* researches the nature of an efficient market. An efficient market would suggest that all market participants receive and act on any relevant information on a company as soon as it becomes available, so that the actual price of a stock at any one time represents it true valuation. This theory also suggests that there is no such thing as a "hot tip" (outside of illegal inside information) since any information that an individual investor may garner about a company has already been learned, considered, and acted upon in the markets by market professionals. Furthermore, it suggests that the information is already reflected in the stock price.

Malkiel's book uses the efficient market basis to propose his "random walk theory," also known as the efficient market hypothesis (EMH). According to EMH, the price of stocks follow a random path up and down, making it impossible to predict with any accuracy which direction the stock will move at any point. Both of these theories are somewhat controversial, of course, because they suggest that the thousands of market analysts and forecasters (many paid in the millions of dollars per year) are not important.

But the theory has been tested many times. "More than 30 years ago, *Forbes* magazine invested in 28 stocks ($1,000 each) pegged by darts on a stock-market page. The portfolio grew 370% over 17 years, far exceeding the growth of the general market and almost all professional money managers."[2] Since this early test, the concept has been retested hundreds of times, sometimes using outrageous methods such as having monkeys pick stocks randomly out of a newspaper. The results have consistently performed in a general bell-shaped curve around the market performance mean.[3]

Further evidence to support this theory is the tremendous success of stock index funds. An index is a benchmark that measures financial performance. A stock index is an index of market prices of a particular group of stocks, such as the Standard and Poors 500 (S&P 500). (The S&P 500, a market-value weighted index of five hundred blue-chip stocks, is considered to be the benchmark in determining the overall performance for the stock market.) Finally, a stock index fund is simply a mutual fund whose portfolio, and ultimately its performance, mirrors a stock index (in many cases, the S&P 500 specifically).

The reason stock index funds have become so popular is because of their simplicity and their superior performance. While thousands of high-paid Wall Street managers live and breathe financial news, pour over data, buy high-priced research, fly to visit companies directly, and always look for an edge in finding the perfect stock, *still less than 20*

percent of mutual fund managers can beat the S&P 500 index benchmark.
This fact supports the controversial efficient market hypothesis.

A few years ago I met a young Harvard graduate named Mary Naber. She was working on an academic publication to support the notion that investors who actively screened their portfolios for offensive companies would not have to sacrifice rate of return. Her paper, "Investing with Catholic Principles," evaluated the effects of portfolio divestment by assessing the significance between a screened-portfolio's risk-adjusted value and equally weighted rates of return. She concluded that investing with Catholic principles should not lead to a diminished rate of return potential:

> The main point here is that if you choose two different stocks with similar risk characteristics (something we know, which is measured by beta [a stock's volatility in relation to the S&P 500's beta of 1.0]), one stock is no better or worse a deal than the next stock. The significance to you, the thoughtful investor, is that if the university professors are correct and the EMH is true, your returns should not be adversely affected in Values-Based Investing. Of course your broker or financial advisor will probably argue that by excluding morally offensive companies, you might miss out on some phenomenal returns (due to the limited universe). The EMH says that the sinful company is no more likely to gain 12% than a more decent one with the same beta risk, because any advantage has already been recognized and arbitraged away.[4]

HISTORICAL EVIDENCE FROM THE MARKETPLACE

Perhaps the best evidence that values-based investors do not need to sacrifice rate of return comes from the historical evidence already gathered from the more socially liberal world of socially responsible investing. As I discussed in chapter 2 and will discuss more in chapter 8, the SRI community has been active in screened investing years ahead of the Christian community. Using the lessons already learned, we can come to some clear conclusions. One of them is that screening investments does not lead to diminished rates of return.

Specifically, SRI pioneer Amy Domini began her career in 1984 when she and Peter Kinder coauthored a book, *Ethical Investing: How to Make Profitable Investments without Sacrificing Your Principles.* They preached two basic premises. First, every investment in stocks or in savings accounts has an ethical dimension. Secondly, investors can and should apply their ethical standards to potential investments.[5]

Her methodology of screening out investments using personal convictions is generally the same as VBI but differs on the definitions of the screens used; her methods focus on socially liberal motives. Nevertheless, the evidence of SRI is compelling to Christians who may worry about facing the choice of either sacrificing rate of return or sacrificing their principles with their investments.

After years of pioneering the social investing movement, Domini worked to create a socially responsible stock index designed to track the performance of socially screened investments and compare it to that of the market as a whole. As we discussed earlier, investors often use stock indexes to gauge the overall health of a market. The most famous of the indexes is the Dow Jones Industrial Average, which is derived very simply by adding up the prices of the thirty stocks that make up the index. The total value of the thirty stock prices equals the Dow Jones index for that day.

Domini recognized that to be taken seriously on Wall Street, socially responsible investors would have to create a similar index that represented only socially acceptable companies based on the social screens they employed, for example, anti-pollution and anti-nuclear criteria. They chose to mirror the most prestigious index, the Standard and Poors 500. According to cofounder Peter Kinder, "If the index wasn't accepted by the institutions, we'd be marginalized forever. Therefore, we made the Domini primarily an index of large corporations that institutions favor. We started with the S&P 500 and ended up with about 250 of these companies that passed our screens. Then we screened the next-largest companies until we had added another hundred. Finally we included 50 smaller companies with notably strong social performances."[6]

On May 1, 1990, the Domini 400 Social Index was born. Though money came into the fund very slowly at first, the Domini 400 index began to surprise the establishment on Wall Street. By the mid-'90s, the facts were indisputable that social screening did not degrade investment performance. The latest annual performance comparisons are:

Year	Domini Socially Screened Index	Standard and Poor's 500 Index
1992	12.10%	7.68%
1993	6.54%	10.08%
1994	-0.36%	1.26%
1995	35.17%	37.50%
1996	21.84%	23.07%
1997	36.02%	33.40%
1998	32.99%	28.58%
1999	22.63%	21.04%

As of March 31, 2000, the average annual rate of return for the Domini socially screened index since its inception ten years earlier was 19.55 percent versus the nonscreened Standard and Poor's 500 average of 19.13 percent.[7]

This comparison is historical fact and not just classroom theory, and it is information that the Christian community must take to heart. The indisputable evidence is that there is no reason to believe an investor must compromise rate of return when choosing to invest with his convictions. This conclusion is summarized in a statement by money manager Thomas Van Dyck: "Once the research on the correlation between social investing and long-term performance becomes widely known, I believe the vast majority of Americans will want their investments not only to make money, but also to work for what they believe."[8]

QUESTIONING THE ROLES AND RESPONSIBILITIES OF THE CHRISTIAN INVESTOR

I believe that the evidence is quite clear. Unfortunately, the evidence is not well known. Over the years, I have been amazed by the number of Christian ministries, pro-life organizations, church denominations, college foundations, and endowments that have summarily dismissed the notion of screening investments due to their perception that it would cut their rate of return.

In fact, only once in my twelve-year career as a financial counselor did I come across a Christian leader who proactively took responsibility for the kinds of companies his organization would invest in. I was making a presentation to a small regional board of trustees for the Nazarene Church. We were discussing the kinds of items expected in an investment proposal, such as asset allocation, fees, and expenses. The church superintendent asked me, "Can you assure me that none of the companies in these mutual funds you are recommending would be offensive to our church members?"

"No, I cannot," I responded. "Mutual funds are large portfolios that are very difficult to track, and I simply don't have time to identify what every company does to protect your church members."

Other board members quickly added to my explanation with comments like, "He's right. It's just too hard to do," and "Nobody else can do that, so we shouldn't worry about it either."

What impressed me about that church superintendent was his sincerity in challenging me and his board members: "Maybe it's tough, and maybe nobody else does it, but does that take away our responsibility to do it if it's the right thing to do? Just because nobody else thinks that it is important enough, should we adopt that as our own standard?"

His statement convicted me. I knew that many financial institutions demanded such accountability when it came to issues like environmental protection, nuclear power, weapons production, and other socially liberal issues. In fact, various colleges, federal employee pension plans, and institutional investors were already demanding that their portfolios be cleansed of companies involved in such issues.

I wondered why Christians and other people of faith chose to demand less accountability of companies involved in substantive issues that affect the family.

I knew that those representing socially responsible investing parameters had attracted billions of dollars of capital from people and organizations that felt so strongly about their personal convictions that they used social screening in their investments. Resources like the Domini socially screened index were becoming successful because the number of investors seeking screening tools was growing. In fact, some nonprofit groups were recognizing that in order to fulfill their charters, they had a responsibility to screen investments on behalf of their donors.

Once again, I wondered: Why don't Christians have even more passion to avoid being a part of companies involved in pornography or in the marketing of blood, gore, and sex to young children? Why aren't Christians even more outraged at potential profit from companies in the business of abortion?

And why don't the boards of directors and the professionals involved in managing investment portfolios for Christian organizations scrutinize the cultural values of the companies they own as closely as they do the financial value?

FINDING THE SAME ANSWER FROM TWO DIFFERENT PATHS

In coming to terms with these questions, I concluded that Christians absolutely should, and must, consider screening investments for which they are personally or professionally accountable. I reached this conclusion by following different analytical paths.

PROFESSIONAL INVESTMENT PROTOCOL

First, an investment professional is trained to understand and abide by a fundamental standard referred to as "fiduciary responsibility." This is the professional term for being accountable for prudent investment decisions in line with the objectives of the investor. For example, a professional would violate this fiduciary responsibility if he invested a widow's only financial "nest egg" in risky aggressive investments. Similarly, a professional would violate this fiduciary responsibility just as much by investing the money of an aggressive long-term investor only in a low-interest-bearing money market account. In either case, the investment manager has failed to prudently create a portfolio consistent with the specific needs and objectives of the individual investor.

It is interesting that the socially responsible investing movement has actually been challenged using this very obligation. There is a school of thought, and even a history of some litigation, that investment managers who use social screening actually violate their fiduciary responsibility to the investor. The argument states that by reducing the universe of available securities via screening there will be an inherent and needless limitation of financial reward opportunity, thus leading to a violation of fiduciary responsibility.

This argument has not held water. It is a two-dimensional argument in a three-dimensional world. It does not acknowledge that to certain investors the need for clean investing can be just as important as the need for superior financial performance.

However, by adding this third dimension, it must be concluded that an investment manager also has a fiduciary responsibility to recognize and consider the values of the investor he represents in making investment choices. For example, the investment manager of a church denomination absolutely violates a professional fiduciary responsibility if he or she invests church money into a company like Tenet Healthcare (NYSE symbol THC). Tenet has hospital properties that facilitate for-profit elective abortions. Another example would be the World Wide Wrestling Federation (NASDAQ symbol WWFE), which sells extreme violence laced with eroticism directly to children.

BIBLICAL FOUNDATION AND AUTHORITY

Second, what better authority is there than the Bible to answer these questions? Many Scriptures speak to the need for obedience in the stewardship of money. Are financial returns and cultural values mutually exclusive when it comes to our investments?

In Ephesians, Paul wrote from prison about God's eternal purpose to establish and complete his body, the church of Christ, and discussed the position of believers as well as the practices of believers. Specifically, I believe Paul gives clear answers to the obligations we have:

> Be imitators of God, therefore, as dearly loved children and live a life of love, just as Christ loved us and gave himself up for us as a fragrant offering and sacrifice to God.
>
> But among you there must not be even a hint of sexual immorality, or of any kind of impurity, or of greed,

because these are improper for God's holy people. Nor should there be obscenity, foolish talk or coarse joking, which are out of place, but rather thanksgiving. For of this you can be sure: No immoral, impure or greedy person—such a man is an idolater—has any inheritance in the kingdom of Christ and of God. Let no one deceive you with empty words, for because of such things God's wrath comes on those who are disobedient. Therefore do not be partners with them.

For you were once darkness, but now you are light in the Lord. Live as children of light (for the fruit of the light consists in all goodness, righteousness and truth) and find out what pleases the Lord. Have nothing to do with the fruitless deeds of darkness, but rather expose them." (Ephesians 5:1–11 NIV)

When considering whether to become an owner of a company like Tenet Healthcare or World Wide Wrestling Federation, can the mandate be any clearer? Paul states, "Therefore, do not be partners with them. . . . Have nothing to do with the fruitless deeds of darkness, but rather expose them."

Finally, as much of this chapter already illustrated, there is no empirical or analytical reason to believe that culturally clean investments result in any less financial performance than those that profit from anti-family products and policies. Whether you examine academic analysis and theories or proven history in the marketplace, screening investments using your personal convictions does not necessarily mean you will make less money. There is no doubt that you do not have to compromise on your rate of return in order to not compromise on your personal values when it comes to your investment portfolio.

No matter how you analyze it, the conclusion is the same. The Nazarene superintendent I encountered years ago was correct. A professing Christian investor or a professional investment manager who invests on behalf of Christians must accept the consideration of values-based investing as an integral fiduciary responsibility in the investment selection and management process with just as much gravity as he does the ultimate financial performance.

CHAPTER 8

SRI:
SAME VISION —
DIFFERENT VALUES?

The church was not formed to manage the property of its members, or to command their charitable efforts; nor can it show any commission to that effect. You are a steward not for the church, but for God. The property which you have, or may have in possession, belongs to you; as an individual and not as a member of the church; and you as an individual, must account for it to the supreme proprietor.
LEONARD BACON,
The Christian Doctrine of Stewardship (1832)

I HAD JUST BEEN INTRODUCED to the concept of socially responsible investing for the first time after hearing a representative for the Calvert Mutual Fund Group speak. He claimed that his mutual funds invested for profit while screening out companies that were socially irresponsible. I remember wondering, *Who gave them the right to define what is socially responsible and what is socially irresponsible?*

Since I was living in Washington state at the time, I was especially sensitive that he singled out Boeing as an example. I challenged him, "I happen to believe that helping provide for the national defense is perhaps the essence of social responsibility." Of course, Calvert screened Boeing from its portfolios because the company had contracts with the Department of Defense.

Since that day I have wondered many times why Wall Street or the mainstream business press has never challenged, not once, such definitions of what is good for our country's society and culture under the name of socially responsible investing. What defines social responsibility and social irresponsibility? How did the accepted definition of socially responsible investing become so widely accepted?

HISTORY OF THE SRI MOVEMENT

Many of those who represent the socially responsible investing business will not give accurate credit to the fact that its roots are in the Christian Church. As early as the 1800s, the Quakers withdrew from business relationships and partnerships involved in the slave trade. In the 1920s, churches and denominations in America chose to actively screen their money from being invested in "sin stocks," defined then as belonging to companies that manufactured products related to alcohol, tobacco, and gambling.

The movement was narrow in scope and did not thrive for years. The Catholic Church was most dominant in its early days. Wall Street never even noticed the movement. Then the Vietnam War and the social anarchy of the 1960s emerged among the country's youth and college campuses.

Social leftists quickly recognized the investment community in general and SRI specifically as new tools that could be used to promote their activist agendas. The church-based SRI agenda was co-opted quickly with a revolutionary fervor that reflected the mood and agenda of the 1968 Democratic National Convention in Chicago. Just as social leftists seized the political power and leadership of the Democratic Party in 1968, the same leftists began to take leadership and control of economic power through the SRI movement.

The first SRI mutual fund was launched during the height of the Vietnam protests in 1971. The Pax World Fund, known as a "peace-oriented" fund, became the first mutual fund to offer screened invest-ments on a broad range of social issues.[1] Other new mutual funds built on social activism were Dreyfus Third Century, Calvert, Working Assets, and Parnassus funds. Mainstream business writers and Wall Street analysts scoffed at and ignored these early efforts.

A few religious denominations added legitimacy to the changing face of the movement. The left-leaning Unitarian Universalist Church group was among the first. In 1970, the UUA Board of Trustees took a stand that 5 percent of its endowment funds should be put into "alternate investments"—community loan funds.[2] Community loan funds were designed to be monies that allowed certain groups to get preferential access to loans if the group was either recognized as socially disadvantaged or if the group was promoting a "socially responsible" agenda such as wetlands preservation. The group's policies were to not invest in tobacco companies, companies with more than 5 percent investment in weapons production, companies that blatantly polluted the environment, or companies with blatant discriminatory policies.

LEFTIST ROOTS

In 1971, the National Council of Churches (NCC) formed a com-mittee on investments to review such policies and their role among the churches the NCC represented. At the time, the NCC represented between thirty-five and forty million Protestants. The organization was investigating how it could use the tenets of the SRI movement to advance its agenda. When the NCC jumped on the social screening bandwagon, it was a tremendous boost for the new image of the movement.

However, the NCC was extremely controversial among evangelical Christians at the time. Many claimed that the NCC's role was too political and not focused enough on evangelism. The NCC was criti-cized for ignoring the gospel message.

Critics cited many examples:

- The NCC issued a press release that said in most people's minds there was no longer any conflict between the teachings of the Bible and those of Charles Darwin. The release cited weekly NCC telecasts, "which accept and explain the theory of evolution." It said that heavy mail from viewers showed that "scarcely one in a thousand still finds any conflict between the Darwinian theory and the Book of Genesis."[3]

- The NCC Broadcasting and Film Commission published a story that said: "What about hell? What's happened to the fires which preachers used to threaten the wicked? What's happened is that most of us are now quite unwilling and unable to say that God chooses to send any of His creatures to a place of endless and limitless torture . . . . So (hell) is not a place He sends men to, but a condition that they choose."[4]

- "In a special issue of the *International Journal of Religious Education,* the official publication of the NCC Division of Christian Education, Gerald A. Larue said that the message of the Bible is merely 'the witness of a writer at some point in history. We need not agree with what he (the writer) says, but we can appreciate his point of view.'"[5]

- A pamphlet titled "Called to Responsible Freedom: The Meaning of Sex in the Christian Life" by William Graham Cole, published by the NCC for United Christian Youth Movement, said, "What justifies and sanctifies sexuality is not the external marital status of the people before the law, but rather what they feel toward each other in their hearts."[6]

The NCC investment committee that was formed in 1971 turned into the Interfaith Center for Corporate Responsibility (ICCR). The center began small and reached out to churches as a way to grow and gain clout and support. Today the ICCR has more than 275 member churches and/or church organizations and acts as a clearinghouse and strategy center for various social issue campaigns. Institutional members of the ICCR represent Protestant, Catholic, and Jewish faiths.

Supporters of the movement began to add new and broader screen definitions to the traditional SRI screens. These early screens were predominantly focused on environmental polluters, companies with business ties to South Africa (because of the apartheid policies of the ruling government), defense, and nuclear power. While these additions were just a taste of the complex lists to come, they signaled a radical departure from the church's earlier attempts to avoid sin stocks.

By the late 1970s, SRI activism had split into two methodologies, both of which served to fulfill the same purpose. First, "avoidance screening" referred to the traditional approach that social screening had always taken—cleaning out the "undesirable" companies that one wished to not be a part of. By avoiding these companies in the first place, a portfolio was "clean" of offensive businesses. Perhaps more importantly, investors also denied these companies access to their money, or capital, for them to conduct their business. Avoidance screening is what social screening had always been.

However, SRI activists also created a new level of screening they referred to as "affirmative screening"—the process of actually searching out those companies that are promoting the values with which one agrees. In this instance, SRI affirmative screening initially sought out those companies that promoted energy efficient, clean-burning, and non-nuclear power. Companies that invested in wind power, solar power, hydrogen power, and battery-driven cars were considered more deserving of investment dollars because their personal philosophies conformed to SRI key social criteria.

Using this two-pronged approach, the movement had two main purposes. First, it was to "divert capital away from destructive uses by refusing to invest in businesses or institutions which pollute, use unfair labor practices, conduct businesses in oppressive regimes, produce nuclear weapons or nuclear power, or employ other damaging practices." Second, it was to "channel capital toward socially responsible purposes by investing in companies and institutions whose products, services and practices contribute to a sustainable society."[7] (For a complete review of common SRI screens found with both "avoidance" and "affirmative" methodologies, please refer to the appendix.)

In the early 1980s, a number of formal organizations and groups followed the path of the ICCR. In 1982, a single mother and social activist named Joan Bavaria founded the Social Investment Forum, an organization designed to represent the SRI industry as a whole.[8] In 1984, Amy Domini wrote her ground-breaking book on the SRI movement and began to grow her asset management company—Kinder, Lydenburg, Domini & Company—to support her new socially screened mutual funds.

On May 1, 1990, Domini and her firm created the Domini 400 Social Index. By the mid-'90s, social screening showed it could generate significant investment fees for those companies that wished to market its products.

According to a press release from the Social Investment Forum, as of the end of 1999, more than $2 trillion in investments in the United States used some form of socially responsible screens. The figure represented an increase of more than 82 percent from 1997 levels.[9] Over the course of the 1990s, the growth in socially screened mutual funds grew significantly as well. In 1983, there were only twelve socially screened mutual funds. By the beginning of the year 2000, there were seventy-three available to the public.

Overall, the goal of modern socially responsible investing and the agendas it represents can be summed up by a quote from a leading SRI advocacy group called Co-Op America: "Taken together, these invest-ment strategies encourage companies to take account of the social and environmental costs of doing business . . . . The ripple effect of respon-sible investing will build into a wave that will ultimately see the finan-cial market banking on corporations that promote a just and sustain-able society. One day destructive companies may pay the price in lower stock prices and higher cost of capital; and they will be driven out of business. When that happens, the world will profit from an economy at work for the people and the planet."[10]

A NEW WORLDVIEW

Socially responsible investing of the present day obviously has very little in common with the vision originally intended by the Quakers in the 1920s and the Catholic nuns of the 1960s. While many of the issues represented in both the avoidance and the affirmative screens are noble, they certainly represent a liberal political theme.

The leading SRI think tank in America today, the ICCR has a politically and theologically liberal heritage. Today's SRI methodology reflects a distinctly different agenda from modern evangelical concerns when it comes to presenting a message of determining screening crite-ria for companies and investments.

According to an ICCR statement,

> ICCR vigorously challenges corporations to make peace and social justice concerns part of the decision-making formula in business. Churches in America are stewards of billions of dollars of stocks and bonds in pensions and endowments. Members of the ICCR (churches, dioceses, and religious communities) accept the unique challenge of addressing issues of corporate responsibility with our resources, particularly our investments.

> Our covenant is to work ecumenically for justice in
> and through economic structures, and for stewardship of
> the earth and its resources. We publish *The Corporate
> Examiner* ten times yearly—reviewing publications and
> media, presenting opinions and ideas, and examining
> U.S. church and corporate policies and actions on
> nuclear weapons, environment, foreign investment,
> minorities and women, health, hunger, energy, human
> rights, and alternative investments.[11]

Leaders at ICCR and other leading advocates of the socially responsible investing methodology have referred to the practice as "natural investing." This leap is significant because it transcends the practical application of screening investments to be consistent with one's values and represent one's theology. Values-based investors presuppose the value of avoiding investment in business that defiles the Word of God and is contrary to scriptural teachings. Likewise, SRI advocates, or natural investors, use the same economic models with their own presupposition of the value of humanity, protecting Mother Earth and seeking a human justice based on economic fairness doctrines.

Natural investors and SRI advocates as a whole have a dramatically different worldview from evangelical Christians. While the strategies they use to promote their respective agendas are built on the same basic economic models, the desired goals and results are extremely different.

Natural investing advocate and author Cliff Feigenbaum has written about the underlying theology.

> The incredible power and fruits of the idea that the
> world, and the cosmos, is a machine and that God is the
> master watchmaker kept our doubts at bay for over two
> centuries. Eventually, cracks in this worldview began to

appear. . . . Throughout all these centuries, and into the present time, native cultures and many Westerners have maintained a more natural view of the world. . . . Their worldview has served as the foundation for a wide variety of successful social systems and richly satisfying personal lives. Indeed, the "new" Natural Worldview is, in many ways, simply a modern integration of traditional native wisdom. . . . The principles of nature have guided the successful evolution of life on Earth for over four billion years. The Natural Worldview is proving relevant to every field of human endeavor, as scientists continue to glean new insights from their study of living systems.[12]

The theology underlying mainstream SRI agendas as articulated by natural investing uncovers the root of the differences between socially responsible investing and values-based investing. More than tools of activism, models of capitalistic influence, and public relations strategies to influence corporations, the two investment screening tools at their heart boil down to the theological goals they attempt to reach.

Our culture's dominant view today is that life is all there is and that nature is all we need to explain everything that exists. This is the philosophy of naturalism, widely accepted in the secular world. Naturalism states that in the beginning there were particles and natural laws. Nature created the universe out of nothing, that nature formed our planet, and that nature acted through Darwinian mechanisms to evolve complex life-forms and, finally, human beings with the marvels of consciousness and intelligence.[13]

Compare this with the Bible: "In the beginning God created the heavens and the earth" (Gen. 1:1).

Charles Colson identifies these exact distinctions as a key in the present-day culture war. "The real battle is worldview against worldview, religion against religion. On one side is the naturalistic worldview, claiming that the universe is the product of blind, purposeless forces. On the other side stands the Christian worldview, telling us we were created by a transcendent God who loves us and has a purpose for us." He adds, "The Christian worldview begins with the Creation, with a deliberate act by a personal Being who existed from all eternity. This personal dimension is crucial for understanding Creation. Before bringing the world into existence, the Creator made a choice, a decision: He set out a plan, an intelligent design."[14]

The two worldviews couldn't be more different. Despite the similarities and congruencies of socially responsible investing and values-based investing, the true agendas behind each remain a world apart.

Yet these distinctions are not recognized or understood by the vast majority of the well-intentioned investing public. In fact, leaders of the SRI movement have aggressively sought the acceptance of the religious community. In the promotion of noble causes like environmental preservation and a hope for peace on Earth, SRI leaders have tried to shave off the sharp radical edges and promote a nonthreatening image of planetary citizenship to the public.

Of course, it is in the best interest of the SRI community to attract as broad a group as it can in marketing its products. Money managers who integrate SRI screening in their portfolios are usually compensated with a management fee based on a percentage of the portfolio being managed. The more money an SRI manager can attract, the more money the manager earns in fees. This is certainly one reason SRI leaders have tried to package a leftist agenda behind the centrist theme of simply being environmentally friendly. Who can argue against wanting clean air and water?

A brilliant tactic used to mainstream the SRI agenda was to rename the movement in selected circles as "ethical investing." This term is often used when marketing traditional SRI screening services and products to the religious community. Guess what? The plan works. It is estimated that at least $1.25 billion from religious institutions, endowments, denominations, and retirement plans is invested using SRI screening.[15]

Ethical investing, and the naturalism theology at its core, is a siren tempting Christian institutions and people of faith to embrace it in an attempt to feel good by doing good.

Don't be fooled, however. Two conclusions from this examination can be reached. First, the strategy and effectiveness of screened investing is a desirable path for Christians to follow in an attempt to uplift our culture in obedience to God and to live his will in all aspects of our lives. Second, the underlying agenda represented by mainstream socially responsible investing, otherwise known as ethical investing or natural investing, is its own theology and worldview that lifts humankind as its own savior.

CHALLENGING THE RHETORIC

As I first understood the true agenda behind the socially responsible investing movement, I was exasperated that Christians would ever participate in it, endorse it, or even promote it. As I learned more and got to know some of the movement's leaders, I decided to use their own words to prove the need for the Christian-based values-based investing approach in the marketplace.

The fact remains that there is freedom in America to act on one's own personal convictions, whether they are Darwinian, Hindu, or Christian in nature. I fervently agree with the right of Muslims, Buddhists, secular humanists, and others to be able to invest their personal money in businesses that share and represent their own faith and convictions. SRI leaders are often quick to publicly agree with this right.

I saw this basic right as a cornerstone in developing a values-based alternative to the SRI movement. After all, who could argue against pro-life activists having the same right to screen their invest-ments as environmental activists have? The fundamental principle with which I strongly agree in the SRI movement is that individual and professional investors should have the right to avoid investing in businesses that are personally offensive to them. Those of us who supported VBI felt that it could be built on the same fundamental investment principles the SRI movement used. At that point, there was common ground.

When I was first promoting my new values-based investing research firm—Institute for American Values—I often mentioned in my media interviews that cultural conservatives and Christians should have the same convenient access to screening data based on the issues important to them. I always used the SRI movement as an example that conser-vatives and evangelicals should follow.

Reporters often asked me why such a task wasn't simply a duplica-tion of effort, citing such examples as tobacco, alcohol, and gambling. In some cases I was "informed" by reporters that some organizations even screened for abortion. Of course, further examination almost uni-versally found this to mean birth control.

Words have meaning. In some cases, they have more meaning than you can recognize at first glance. This was certainly the case in this instance. The mere fact that "ethical" investing was embraced as an accurate description of socially responsible investing was taken to be literal across fundamentally opposite worldviews. "Ethical" to environ-mentalists may have meant something completely different than it did to Christians. It was the difference between protecting trees and pro-tecting the unborn. Yet the description was never challenged.

Adding to the confusion was the fact that SRI screening included the traditional three sin-stock areas that have been associated as Christian issues: alcohol, tobacco, and gambling. With these three issues in hand and by marketing the word "ethical" through the press nationwide, the leaders of the SRI movement found an open door to the Christian community. They successfully marketed to Christian institutions, ministries, endowments, private school foundations, retirement plans, and individual investors—all in the name of promoting "ethics" or "social responsibility" with their money.

REACTION BY THE PRESS

As I began my personal mission to create an alternative to socially responsible investing that was consistent with a Christian worldview, I was anticipating that I would be embraced by the leaders of the existing SRI industry as an extension of their movement and that I would be spurned by the mainstream press. I was certain that the notion of cultural screening as opposed to social or "ethical" screening would be met with the predictable labels of "extremist" and "radical right" from the traditional media. I was also expecting organizations like the National Right to Life to jump on the bandwagon in recognition that there was a new tool for them to use in the fight for their cause. I was also certain that SRI leaders like Amy Domini would consider values-based investing to broaden their message and extend the acceptance and household recognition of their own products.

I was wrong. The press embraced the vision. The liberal-leaning _Philadelphia Inquirer_ was the first national newspaper to write about my new work. In an article published September 29, 1996, the paper said that when it comes to traditional socially responsible investing "social conservatives have not had as many choices."[16] One month later in a breakthrough article, the _New York Times_ featured values-based investing in its Sunday business section. The _Times_ said, "Socially responsible investing is usually seen as a liberal approach, one intended to avoid supporting companies that pollute, discriminate or profit from war. Now there is a way for investors with a conservative bent to apply their convictions."[17]

In doing the interviews for both the *Inquirer* and the *Times,* I was amazed at how open the writers were toward the fact that Christians and people of faith should have the same opportunity to invest with their personal convictions as do socially liberal investors. I think they were expecting me to raise my fists and call for demonstrations and boycotts. Rather, this was a call for Christians to exercise the same personal rights in their investment choices as anyone else.

With only a few exceptions, I found that national and international newspapers, business magazines, and trade magazines endorsed the need and opportunity for the conservative values-based investing. Curiously, the only major national publication that did not embrace the new idea was the *Wall Street Journal.* After three long telephone interviews with its reporter, I learned the article was never to see the light of day. A few months later I learned that the journalist I spoke with was also moonlighting as a reporter for a gay and lesbian Internet site known as "Planet Out," which possibly explained her motivation for dumping the article. Over the next year, articles in *Mutual Fund* magazine and *Money* magazine endorsed the right for Christians to screen their investments.

Even network television embraced the topic. CNBC asked me to explain the differences between values-based investing and traditional SRI. I was called by one of its producers to appear live on a program with Amy Domini, the recognized pioneer and leader of SRI. She was to appear from a studio in Boston, and I was in a studio in Seattle. CNBC's moderator Ron Ensana introduced me as the "new kid on the block" of issues-based investing.

It was evident that Domini had never heard of my company or values-based investing. I was trying to steer the interview to the common message we both shared—the right of investors to invest in a way consistent with their own personal convictions, regardless of what those convictions are. Domini chose to focus on the fact that my filters screened out the Walt Disney Company. She seemed to suggest that because a family-friendly movement like mine would screen out Disney, our process lacked credibility.

A CASE STUDY: THE MMA PRAXIS FUND

An example of how Christians are being misled about the real SRI agenda involves the MMA Praxis Fund. Through funds like Praxis, thousands of Christian investors falsely believe that SRI, called ethical investing, screens for issues like abortion and pornography.

These perceptions were demonstrated to me through an interesting course of events. I was appearing as a guest on a syndicated national Christian radio talk show called "Crosstalk," based at WCVY in Milwaukee, Wisconsin. The host allowed listeners to call in with questions. One of the callers asked about the score of the MMA Praxis Growth Fund. It seemed to be a simple question, but the specific fund represented a number of implications.

First, my answer to the question was simple. I consulted my laptop computer to see what our internal report said about the MMA Praxis Growth Fund. I told the caller that the fund "failed" our cultural screens in the areas of abortion, pornography, and homosexuality. The caller responded, "Are you sure?" I repeated the answer. At that time, more than 30 percent of the fund's assets were invested in companies involved in abortion or pornography and companies that specifically promoted homosexuality with their internal policies.

The caller was still mystified how the MMA Praxis Growth Fund could have such a poor record. Why was she so mystified? The fund is sponsored by the Mennonite Mutual Aid Association, self-described as a "fraternal stewardship solutions organization." MMA has more than $1.2 billion of assets under management and has annual revenues of more than $240 million.

It was founded in 1945 by the Mennonite Church as groups of Mennonites put their faith into action by sharing resources with each other. MMA offered loans to those who volunteered to perform fellowship and welfare services organized by the church. As the organization grew, members from other related church denominations began to participate in MMA.

Today, MMA serves twenty-five different Anabaptist Christian denominations, which have their roots in the sixteenth-century Reformation. These include but are not limited to the Bible Fellowship Church, Church of the Brethren, the Conservative Mennonite Conference, the Evangelical Mennonite Church, Evangelical United Brethren, Fellowship of Evangelical Bible Churches, Mennonite Brethren Church, the Society of Friends (Quakers), and the United Christian Church.

Consistent with the obvious mission of the conservative church denominations that it represented, the MMA Praxis Growth Fund is marketed as "the only mutual fund in the U.S. designed to match Anabaptist Christian beliefs through the use of positive screens, shareholder activism, and community development investing."[18] Specifically, the fund's own marketing materials also say that the fund "exists to help individuals meet their financial goals in a way that supports their beliefs."

An average investor reading this marketing language would assume that the fund represents Christian values and beliefs. In other words, this paints a fairly clear picture that the MMA fund philosophy represents a Christian worldview. No wonder the caller was shocked to learn that the fund failed our screening standards.

The caller thanked me and hung up. The rest of the show was uneventful. However, the next day at my office I received a telephone call from an officer with the MMA organization. He told me that MMA had received a number of telephone calls in response to the information I had passed on during the previous day's radio show. He complained that I had called the MMA Praxis Fund a "pro-abortion" fund.

Taken aback slightly, I let him know that the word "pro-abortion" was not used, but the fact that his fund owned companies involved in the business of abortion was absolutely true. He challenged me. After a very brief explanation, he said he disagreed on our definitions. He felt that a company that created insurance policies that paid for elective abortions, even for the reason of sex selection, could not be considered to be promoting abortion. He felt that a company that used company money to financially support Planned Parenthood could not be perceived to be promoting abortion.

He was either naive, uneducated, or pro-abortion. I asked him how MMA could market itself as a Christian-screened fund without embracing such basic filters. The call ended with no conclusions, but he got a clarification of what true values-based investing meant.

A few weeks later he sent me a letter to "adequately address concerns that have been raised surrounding the inclusion of certain companies in the holdings of the MMA Praxis Growth Fund." He said he wanted to "start with an explanation of MMA's SRI methodology."

Of course. MMA has embraced the liberal SRI mantra and philosophy and repackaged it to conservative Christian denominations as a methodology based on Christian guidelines. In fact, the MMA Praxis Growth Fund is a perfect example of a naturalism worldview dressed up and sold as a Christian worldview to thousands of well-meaning Christian investors. An investor in the MMA Praxis Growth Fund is promoting an agenda to protect Mother Earth far more than an agenda to glorify God the Father.

According to the Bible, it is our responsibility to look deeper than the packaging. Christ made it clear that we are called to look closer concerning the cultural implications of our actions. He said, "You hypocrites! You know how to interpret the appearance of the earth and the sky, but you can't interpret these present times" (Luke 12:56).

The letter also said, "Regarding Praxis holding in Hewlett-Packard (related to their support of Planned Parenthood)—While abortion is of significant concern within our customer base, we do not specifically screen against companies supporting Planned Parenthood. MMA recognizes the volume and variety of services provided by this organization in the areas of family planning, as well as prenatal and postnatal care for the poor."

I was speechless at this response. How could he actually expect to carry any credibility as promoting "Anabaptist Christian beliefs" with such a ridiculous statement? Who could agree with the notion that companies like Hewlett-Packard, which supports Planned Parenthood, were not actually supporting abortion but rather simply promoting "family planning"? For example, in 1997, the foundation of Hewlett-Packard founder David Packard sent $843,913 to NARAL—the National Abortion and Rights Action League—to pay for the production and testing of advertisements to promote pro-choice messages on national television. How could anyone interpret this as prenatal and postnatal care for the poor?

Further, the MMA official addressed the screen about promoting homosexuality. "At this time MMA has not taken a position on the issue of benefits to domestic partners. We do believe all people have value and deserve to be treated with dignity and compassion. Furthermore, as a company that derives significant revenue from the sale of health insurance, we believe that the expansion of covered individuals, apart from other issues, is good for business and the general health of our population."

I was amazed at this statement as well. A quick analysis shows that MMA believed any position not supporting homosexuality as a legitimate lifestyle was synonymous with *not* believing that "all people have value and deserve to be treated with dignity and compassion." I was very offended by his comment, as I believe all Christians should be.

Also, his implication that expanding health benefits coverage to domestic partners was good for the "general health of our population" was outrageous and hollow.

The letter ended by saying, "I hope this information is helpful in clarifying both MMA's approach to socially responsible investing and our stance on specific issues of concern." Oh, yes, it was. But unwitting Christians every day are being drawn into this fund and others like it that actually promote a socially liberal naturalism worldview while marketing themselves as a conservative fund with a Christian worldview.

For example, MMA defines its approach: "Stewardship investing is a philosophy of financial decision making motivated and informed by faith convictions . . . . We consider stewardship investing as an intrinsic part of who we are as people celebrating God's generosity and actively following the example of Jesus Christ . . . . Stewardship investing grows out of a 500 year-old Anabaptist faith tradition."

"We seek out companies that support positive values such as the respect for human dignity, responsible management, and environmental stewardship while avoiding industries and activities like gambling, alcohol and tobacco production, and military contracting." MMA ends its definition of stewardship investing by saying that it "challenges us to identify and consistently apply the values we hold dearest. It is an approach that moves beyond philanthropy or simply doing the right thing. Stewardship investing is born of a spirit of thanksgiving which embodies our abiding concern for others."[19]

Evidently, it doesn't have a concern for the unborn or for families who want to protect the biblical definition of families. The MMA Praxis Growth Fund is an example of how sophisticated marketing has been able to sell a humanist and naturalist worldview to attract literally billions of dollars from Christian investors.

Just how much money is at stake? According to the Interfaith Center for Corporate Responsibility, just the Christian organizations that are a part of its organization "hold a total of about $90 billion in their pension funds and other investment portfolios."[20]

SEEKING MY INVITATION

While it was more evident to me than ever that SRI and values-based investing represented diametrically opposed worldviews, I felt there was value in seeking a coalition of the two movements. I felt that it was my turn to ask for a seat at the table of the SRI industry leaders. The two movements did share one overriding and common message: Every individual investor should have the opportunity to invest in a way that is consistent with his or her personal convictions.

Such a coalition would broaden the influence and acceptance of that principle. By joining a general cause of investment screening side by side with SRI, a distinction would be created between SRI and values-based investing. This distinction would force an accurate depiction of what SRI stood for so that it would actually serve the constituents who shared its naturalism worldview, and only them. Christians and people of faith would have a choice on the investment screening menu that would fit their own worldview. It seemed to me to be an obvious step for the maturation of the industry. It would also force the SRI community to discontinue marketing its agenda in stealth to conservative Christians.

I began by contacting leaders of the SRI movement to introduce myself and by attending SRI conferences. I met with Susan Davis, president of the Capital Missions Company and leader of the annual "Making a Profit While Making a Difference" Conference. I also spoke directly with Tim Smith, executive director of the Interfaith Center for Corporate Responsibility. In our conversations, I discussed my intent on seeking a coalition of efforts to jointly promote the theme that people should be able to invest in a way consistent with their own personal convictions. We discussed the distinctions between the SRI and the values-based investing methodologies. At first, with Smith, Davis, and others, I received no initial discouragement from moving ahead.

However, after attending a few conferences and beginning to get attention, it became obvious that some leaders of the movement were in a frenzy about my efforts to associate with them. It was obvious that I was the first person who did not agree with their social beliefs to ever try to join their movement. It was even more obvious that evangelical Christians were not invited to their party. Specifically, I learned that one of the movement's leaders and pioneers had attacked me and my company in a letter.

A friend of mine, who was an SRI insider, passed a copy of the letter to me. In the letter, the SRI advocate lamented that since SRI promoters had "fought for over 20 years for equal opportunities for all people, regardless of race, religion, or sexual preference" it would be inconceivable to open the doors to values-based investing. Also, the letter writer was alarmed that the rights of "gay, lesbian, bisexual, and transgender people" would be taken away if values-based investing was accepted by the group and regarded cultural screening to be the same as "cultural cleansing."

Ironically, the letter represented the kind of intolerance and hatred that SRI claimed to condemn. Clearly, values-based investing does not deny the rights of gay, lesbian, bisexual, or transgendered people to invest with their own convictions in any way. The hateful reference to "cultural cleansing" was a mean-spirited and unwarranted attack on Christians who simply seek the same opportunities that SRI investors already have. I was shocked.

This same theme continued in my attempts to work with SRI leaders. In preparation to attend a conference called "SRI in the Rockies," I ran into more clear messages. The meeting was to be held at the famous Chateau Lake Louise in Alberta, Canada. Originally, I was told that I had to pay the required amount to be recognized as an official conference sponsor. However, when I phoned to find out where to send my sponsorship check, I was told that no more sponsorship slots were available. No reason was ever given. In fact, the conference organization had control of all the rooms and would not offer me a room. My only alternative was to book a small hotel down the road.

It became so evident at the conference that my presence was unwelcome that I said to myself, "Now I know what Rosa Parks felt like." That famous African American refused to move to the back of a city bus in 1955, pressing on in spite of the intolerance around her. Because of the Christian worldview and moral standards that values-based investing represented, I also was being spurned and disrespected, unwelcome at every turn.

Finally, I was able to meet with the two leaders of the group hosting the conference. After a lengthy discussion, the president of the group finally said to me, "Scott, I'm afraid that indeed we are quite hypocritical. The fact is that we really only care about a person's right to screen their investments when their philosophy is the same as ours. I'm sorry, but nobody wants you here. There is no interest in working with values-based investing here."

I appreciated his candor. My assumptions had been validated. The SRI movement was not at all a movement about rights. It was only a movement about promoting a specific liberal agenda hidden behind the rhetoric of individual rights.

The SRI leader's comments also confirmed to me that the present socially responsible investing movement is no home for Christians, people of faith, and the billions of dollars they wish to invest to do the Lord's will. I hold no animosity toward the SRI movement, but I am quick to point out the dramatic differences between its worldview and Christianity's.

CHAPTER 9

DOES VBI WORK? UNDERSTANDING THE CULTURAL COST OF CAPITAL

A market is the combined behavior of thousands of people responding to information, misinformation, and whim.
KENNETH CHANG

ON WALL STREET, the cost of capital is defined as the rate of return that an investor or company would receive if invested elsewhere with the same amount of risk. And on Wall Street, capital is everything.

To further explain, let me use a small business as an example. If you have ever opened your own business, known someone who has, or have even dreamed of doing it yourself, you know that the first big hurdle is finding the money you need to start the business. Your options, if you don't have the money yourself, are a bank, a friend, a family relative, or a venture capitalist if your business idea is big enough.

Assuming you find someone to loan you this money, otherwise known as capital, the amount of interest you will pay will be based largely on the risk determined by the person loaning you the money. Risk is judged by such variables as your experience at operating such a business, your credit rating, and the strength of the market you are

109

entering. For example, if you are opening a restaurant in an area that is already saturated with restaurants, there will be a higher perceived risk, and you will have to pay a higher rate of interest on your money.

The rate of interest that you pay is known as your "cost of money." The higher the rate of interest, the higher the cost of your loan is. At some point, the interest can be so high that your business venture is simply no longer viable.

The same principles hold true for companies that count their earnings in the billions. Access to capital is always of extreme importance. Capital is always needed for new facilities, expansion, inventory, and other costs. A higher cost of capital to the company means that money will have to be used to pay interest rather than to pay for other company operations. In other words, a higher cost of capital means a lower profit margin for the company.

Because of this, generally a company will do everything it can in order to keep its cost of capital as low as possible. One of the key factors for any public company in getting access to capital is the price of its stock. The higher the stock is, the easier it is for a company to get access to new capital.

Here is a simplified example. If your company needed to raise $10 million for expansion, one of your options is to issue new common stock to the public. If the price of your stock was $100 per share, you would have to issue only 100,000 shares of new stock to bring in the $10 million you needed. If the price of your stock was only $50 per share, you would have to issue twice as much stock, or 200,000 shares. Of course, the fewer shares you issue, the less the cost to your company.

The important point of this explanation is that as the price of a company's stock lowers, its cost of capital, or the price of getting new money, rises significantly. Companies will do almost anything they can in order to avoid seeing the value of their stock fall, for this and many other reasons.

This is the key to understanding the true leverage that values-based investors yield on Wall Street. If values-based investors can lead the price of a company's stock to drop because of its association with cultural pollution, then the company will be facing a new cost of capital that most have not recognized before: a "cultural cost of capital."

In other words, the increase in their cost of money has nothing to do with traditional measurements of business. Creditworthiness, market risk, economic cycles, or other factors are not the key for this increase in cost. The reason is specifically because enough individuals have recognized a culturally offensive product or policy and have divested themselves from the company or have avoided investing in it in the first place. Cumulatively, this action will lead to fewer investors buying the stock of the company and many investors selling the stock if they held it. This increases selling pressure and lowers buying demand. On the open stock market, this will always pressure the price of the stock to go down, sometimes significantly.

Is it reasonable to believe that investors can influence the price of a company's stock in any significant way? Yes. There are numerous examples. It is the nature of Wall Street for groups to seek every opportunity available to positively influence the price of their stock. These same tools can be used in many cases to negatively influence the price of a stock.

THE STORY OF VIACOM

One example of how individuals can work to influence the price of a stock is the story of the Viacom-Paramount merger.

Viacom is best known as the company that owns the MTV cable channel. In 1994, Viacom began an epic five-month struggle to acquire control of Paramount Communications. Viacom and its colorful billionaire chairman Sumner Redstone weren't the only ones seeking Paramount. They were competing against Barry Diller and his

QVC home-shopping network. Both wanted the Paramount film and television studios, and both coveted the valuable Paramount library of nearly nine hundred movies that included blockbuster titles like *The Firm* and timeless classics like *Sunset Blvd.*

The battle for Paramount became one of Wall Street's hardest fought and longest running sagas. Near the end, Viacom and Redstone appeared to be certain losers. On January 12, 1995, Paramount directors had just turned down the latest purchase bid from Viacom and chose to back a $10 billion merger offer from Diller's QVC network. Four days later, on a Sunday afternoon, Viacom executives met with Robert Greenhill, the chairman of Smith Barney, in a last-ditch effort to brainstorm a way to overcome QVC's bid. Everyone in the meeting knew that Viacom must respond quickly if it had any chance to get Paramount.

The firm could not put up any additional money, stock, or warrants. With few alternatives left, a thirty-five-year-old investment banking "whiz kid" named Michael Levitt described a scheme that just might work. His idea was to issue a new kind of security called a contingent value right (CVR) or "collar." The collar would basically guarantee the value of Viacom's stock to the Paramount shareholders who would receive them as compensation for the merger.

In the terms of the collar, if the stock price of Viacom failed to reach a certain level within three years of the merger, then Viacom would guarantee the Paramount shareholders an additional amount of cash. But if the Viacom stock hit or surpassed the target price, then the collar would cost the company absolutely no additional cash. In effect, the collar was an insurance policy to the Paramount shareholders for the future value of Viacom's stock.

Viacom's Redstone had a legendary reputation for never giving up. He decided to go with Levitt's collar idea and raised the case bid from $104 a share to $107 a share. The move sealed the victory for Viacom.

Redstone and three other Viacom executives retired to New York's posh 21 Club to celebrate their last-minute victory.

The deal brought new risks to Viacom. With the collar, Viacom had to keep the price of its stock high. Failure to do so would risk millions of dollars of additional cash needed to pay Paramount shareholders. To avoid this, Viacom developed a keen strategy to get the stock price to the level it needed.

According to the specifics of the merger agreement, beginning on April 20, 1995, for a ninety-day trading period, the median of all twenty-day moving average prices of its stock would be calculated. If the median of the averages was $48 or more, the collar expired with no further liability to Viacom. If the price were lower than $48 per share, Viacom would pay Paramount the difference between $48 and the lower trading price, in cash or securities. For example, if the median price ended up being $46, or $2 per share less than the $48 target, it would mean that Viacom owed as much as an additional $113 million to Paramount.

These were powerful incentives for Viacom to do everything in its power to make sure its stock price average met the $48 target. In its quest for a strategy to influence the stock price, Viacom turned to one place it felt could provide the leverage it needed. Viacom turned to mutual fund managers.

In what one Wall Street expert, quoted in a *New York Times* article, referred to as "manipulative,"[1] Viacom focused its efforts on throwing a tremendous three-day party to influence some of Wall Street's top mutual fund money managers. They chose the historic and fashionable Four Seasons Biltmore Hotel nestled on the sunny California coastline of Santa Barbara. Clearly, this was not the first time that a company had wooed Wall Street money managers for the benefit of its stock price. However, few of them had gone to such lengths as Sumner Redstone and Viacom.

Beginning on Sunday, February 26, 1995, Viacom hosted a three-day all-expense-paid trip for fifty of the nation's top mutual fund managers, most of whom represented funds with billions in assets. Viacom even leased a fleet of private jets pick up and return all of its guests.

At the party, managers were showered with gifts, entertainment, gourmet food, and visits with MTV celebrities. Company executives managed to spend time with the managers, trying to convince them that their stock was undervalued and was worthy of purchase by the mutual fund managers. The strategy worked, and the average stock price was above forty-eight dollars, saving millions for Viacom.

Certainly, values-based investors cannot afford to fly mutual fund managers to a five-star hotel for a lavish party. However, the relevance of the Viacom story transcends the party. The key is found in identifying one of the most effective strategies in moving a stock price. That strategy revolves around leverage.

For example, to move the price of a stock on the open market requires the transfer (buy or sale) of a large volume of shares. Small individual purchases or sales will be insignificant in moving the price of a stock. This traditionally requires the coordination of thousands of individuals to make the same buy or sale of their stock at the same time in order to move the price of the stock up or down. Of course, this kind of organization is very difficult and perhaps even impossible in some cases.

However, the mutual fund solves this problem. Mutual funds are large pools of money that represent thousands of individual investors who each own a small piece of the pie. The mutual fund hires one professional money manager who then makes investment decisions for the entire portfolio on behalf of the many fund owners (those who have invested money in the fund).

The financial advantage of the mutual fund is that an investor with just a few thousand dollars can own a small piece of dozens of different stocks. This is a far greater diversification than she would be able to afford on her own. It also spreads the risk of market fluctuation across many stocks instead of just a few and is much more economical for the investor.

Here is the lesson for values-based investing. The mutual fund manager is an individual representing thousands of investors. For example, rather than spending the time to convince a few thousand investors to sell their stock in an offensive company, VBI can try to influence just one money manager to sell the tens of thousands of shares of stock on behalf of his customers. This boils the influence down to one decision maker.

Viacom understood this leverage. The fifty money managers invited to Santa Barbara probably represented the financial influence of more than one hundred thousand individual investors. One mutual fund manager's decision can impact tens of thousands of shares. This is the kind of volume required to actually move the price of a stock on Wall Street.

The good news for values-based investors is that to exercise influence you don't need to host a million-dollar party at a Four Seasons resort. An individual investor can influence by taking his money out of the fund and transfering it to a competitor. For the mutual fund manager, the amount of assets, or total dollars, in his fund is everything. To see the threat of a movement leading investors to transfer their money out of his fund is a very compelling influence. It is quite likely that the manager would change the holding in the fund to avoid losing a significant amount of assets. And it is this specific influence that can be the key strategy in getting corporate Goliaths like Walt Disney Company to stop marketing anti-family products.

A STRATEGY TARGETING DISNEY

There are many reasons to be outraged by the products and policies of the Walt Disney Company over the past few years. Many have reacted to Disney's moral degradation by supporting a consumer boy-cott. A statement from the American Family Association said, "Profits from family entertainment products and theme parks are subsidizing Disney's promotion of the homosexual agenda. A boycott—including even their good products—is the only way to impact the company."[2] Although I do not discourage anyone from participating in this boy-cott, I do not believe it is an effective method.

A boycott may make consumers feel good. Because Christians often feel completely powerless against cultural degradation, a boycott can make us feel as if we are at least doing something to fight back. Unfortunately, it is really all about feelings and very little about posi-tive change.

In fact, in 1998, the *Los Angeles Times* wrote a feature article about that year's Disney shareholder meeting. One angle the story covered was the conversations among the board members mocking the effec-tiveness of the boycott. They obviously believed that, despite what oth-ers said, the boycott had no impact on company sales, earnings, or stock price. Beyond giving Christians an outlet to feel good, the boy-cott simply had very little impact in changing the course of Disney's contribution to cultural pollution in our entertainment industry.

Instead, I suggest that focusing on large owners of Disney stock, such as mutual fund managers, would be much more effective in influ-encing the Disney board of directors to change products. By focusing on large sums of money invested in Disney, values-based investors can effectively increase the cultural cost of capital for Disney.

For example, a Los Angeles-based mutual fund company known as the American Funds Family had a number of large mutual funds that owned significant amounts of Disney stock. In fact, its Investment Company of America, Washington Mutual Fund, and others in the fund family collectively owned enough shares to surpass $1 billion worth of stock. By focusing on the decision-making power of three or four mutual fund managers in one company, values-based investors have the potential of influencing more than $1 billion of capital with Disney. Just imagine the impact if the American Funds Family were successfully convinced to sell Disney stock.

I can guarantee you that the market impact on the stock price from the sale of $1 billion of stock would be enormous. It would immediately get the attention of not only Michael Eisner, but every single board member. They would all be able to quantify the loss of market value as the increased cultural cost of capital.

Disney has every legal right in America to create and sell its entertainment products. However, it does not have the right to use your investment money in capitalizing and creating these entertainment products without your knowledge, even if it gets your money through a mutual fund manager. By denying Disney access to your money, you effectively reduce the number of people willing to invest in the company, and consequently, its cost of money, or cultural cost of capital, should increase. This method actually increases the cost of creating vulgar, pornographic, excessively violent, or anti-family entertainment.

Roaring lambs across the country can stop lashing out at Disney just to feel good. Values-based investing unlocks the door to effective influence using Wall Street's own rules of economics. The result of this market strategy is that companies doing business in a way that does not undermine morality and families will have access to your investment capital instead of Disney and companies like it. Not only will your divestiture punish Disney economically, it will reward those companies that are doing business the right way.

Influencing a Mutual Fund Manager

Sure, this strategy sounds appealing. But how can values-based investors actually influence a group like the American Funds managers to sell a company like Disney? Obviously, no one can afford to throw a multimillion-dollar party with private jets like Sumner Redstone did for Viacom. The key to this strategy is recognizing what motivates mutual fund managers and why individual investors are so important to them.

In the world of politics, why do you think many politicians are sensitive to Reverend Jesse Jackson? It seems if Jackson invites them to a reception, asks to meet with them, or calls their office, congressmen and senators all respond immediately. Jesse Jackson appears to have an open door to Capitol Hill. Why?

It isn't because of who Jesse Jackson is as an individual. While he is an accomplished speaker and has a powerful persona, it is not for these reasons either. Those whom Jesse Jackson represents are why he gets so much attention. To solicit Jesse Jackson's support for a politician is recognized to be the equivalent of soliciting the support of millions of his supporters.

Similarly, the key to values-based investing is to represent to Wall Street a block of investment capital held collectively by people of faith across the country. And, you may be surprised by how much mutual fund managers have in common with politicians.

Politicians judge success by how many constituents vote for them instead of their competitors, while mutual fund managers ultimately judge success by how many investors choose to invest in their funds instead of their competitors' funds. Also, once elected, politicians must keep their constituents happy with their voting records in order to stay in office. Similarly, once mutual fund managers are at the helm, they must keep their investors happy with their investment decisions in order to keep their jobs.

There is only one piece of this puzzle that must change in order for this analogy to work as effectively as it could. For the most part, investors judge a mutual fund manager only on the basis of the rate of return produced. There is no evaluation of what the by-products of those investments are. It is the equivalent of ignoring the fact that a factory is filling the air and water with poison by producing popular and attractive products.

Once investors are able to evaluate the cultural impact of their investment choices, mutual fund managers can be more effectively influenced. Remember, it has been clearly demonstrated that investment rate of return and the philosophy of filtering out anti-family investments are not mutually exclusive. Investors can make as much money investing in clean companies as they can by investing in cultural polluters.

I ran across an excellent example of this methodology at a cocktail party in New York. The event was sponsored and hosted by a mutual fund company called Oppenheimer, headquartered in New York's World Trade Center. While I wandered through the crowd, I introduced myself to the manager of one of Oppenheimer's funds that specialized at investing in small companies. The fund had more than $1 billion in it collectively.

Admittedly, I began pumping the manager with questions designed to help me in my research for creating my values-based investing database. I asked the manager a hypothetical question.

"Let's say you ran across a company named Rick's Cabaret. If you don't know, Rick's is a publicly owned chain of nude dancing clubs. Also, assume that this company had a forecasted earnings growth rate of 75 percent per year. In this example, would you consider buying it even though you knew that it was basically a company employing prostitutes to get its earnings?"

He answered, "Of course I would. I am hired by my shareholders with one very specific goal in mind, and that is to make money. Nowhere in the prospectus or in my job description does it allow me to make moral judgments on behalf of my shareholders. I would definitely buy the stock."

I followed his answer with another hypothetical question. "What if you do hold stock of Rick's Cabaret in your portfolio, and its earnings even surpass your forecasts. Let's even say that it is one of your top ten performing stocks in the whole portfolio. What would you do if you learned that shareholders in your fund were leaving and taking millions of dollars with them to one of your competitors, like Fidelity, simply because they were outraged that you owned the stock of a nude dancing company in your portfolio? What then?"

His response was prompt and without hesitation: "Well, I'd dump it, of course."

The message of this conversation is perhaps one of the most important keys in understanding why values-based investing can work effectively to increase the cultural cost of capital for those companies choosing to profit at the expense of our culture. The key is that most Wall Street money managers, unlike all Washington politicians, are really amoral. Their goals are simply not to pursue any personal agenda in their investing decisions other than to earn money and attract more people to put money into the fund they manage.

A principal reason is their personal motivation. Nearly all mutual fund managers are compensated in part for the amount of assets in the mutual funds they manage. A successful mutual fund manager counts his or her annual compensation in seven or eight figures.

As my conversation illustrated, the point of greatest influence with a mutual fund manager is his or her personal compensation. If a fund manager sees any reason that leads investors to leave his mutual fund to go to one of the competitors, it raises serious attention. Referring back to the example of the American Funds and Disney, I can assure you that the managers of those funds have a far greater loyalty to maintaining the asset levels of their funds than they do to the internal policies and agenda of the Disney Company. In other words, for a money manager it is a very easy choice between losing assets of disgruntled customers or removing a stock from an investor's portfolios that is causing the problem.

INFLUENCING CHRISTIAN-BASED PORTFOLIOS

Thousands of large portfolios in the United States are managed to benefit a variety of ministries, church denominations, Christian schools, Christian universities, Christian relief funds, Christian retirement funds, and so forth. The majority of these funds were created by attracting thousands of contributions from donors who believed very deeply in the mission they wanted to support. But no one has taken the responsibility to screen the investments for offensive companies and businesses. In fact, I would submit that the vast majority of those with fiduciary responsibility for managing these funds haven't taken any steps to screen their portfolios in any way.

Collectively there are billions of dollars of investments in Christian-related nonprofit portfolios in this country. Certainly what most of the managers responsible for these portfolios need is simply education to help them understand the impact their decisions may have in protecting our culture and in helping Christians live so as to fulfill the will of Christ. Also, these managers can be effectively influenced by recognizing that donors demand greater accountability for how their money is invested.

In my early years of developing a values-based research database, I often came across ministries that had invested their own money—many times unwittingly—into companies that were profiting from the very activities they were fighting. As briefly mentioned in chapter 6, I was appalled to find out that a national pro-life ministry headquartered in Washington, D.C., had invested its own retirement plan into funds that held stock in direct abortion providers and prolific Planned Parenthood contributors. Even under direct appeal from me, its board seemed unwilling to recognize the magnitude of its problem. Yet when I mentioned this in passing to financial donors of this nonprofit advocacy group, the donors were furious. Many threatened to suspend their contributions.

One particular donor from Morgantown, West Virginia, wrote to the president of the national pro-life ministry. In his letter he said he was distressed to learn that the "organization's retirement fund portfolio contained investments in companies which profit directly from the abortion industry and that when persons in the organization responsible for such investments were confronted with that information they essentially refused to deal with the suggestion that those investments be removed from the fund."

He added, "I find that totally unacceptable. So much so that I will no longer provide monies to support your organizations. . . . I would appreciate hearing from you to know that you take this situation seriously and to learn how you have dealt with it. It would be ludicrous for you to allow it to continue. I pray that if you haven't already done so, you will act without further delay to correct this extremely unacceptable dichotomy."

It takes very little effort for those responsible for the stewardship of billions of dollars that the Lord has blessed their churches, ministries, and schools with to use the capital not only for a prudent rate of return, but also for a prudent cultural impact. It is indefensible for a pro-life organization to be an owner of a company that chooses to profit from elective abortion services. Once again, as I have already demonstrated in earlier chapters, there is no need to compromise the stewardship fulfillment of investment rate of return in order to fulfill the stewardship responsibility of investing in culturally clean companies that will uplift our society and benefit our families.

CHAPTER 10

EARLY VICTORIES— GOOD NEWS FROM WALL STREET

How many rap songs about slicing women's throats does the world really need?
BOB DOLE

FORMER SENATOR BILL BRADLEY, Democrat from New Jersey, was very clear about his feelings on corporate America's cultural pollution. He called for investors to take the fight directly from their homes to the heart of Wall Street. "If you see something that offends you, find out who the sponsor is. Find out who is on the board of directors. Find out where they live, who their neighbors are, their local clubs, churches and synagogues. Send a letter to the members of the board at their homes and ask whether they realize they are making huge profits from the brutal degradation of human beings. Then send a copy of the letter to all of their neighbors and friends."[1]

TAKING ON A MUTUAL FUND GIANT

Like Bradley, millions of individuals in America are ready to stand up to the cultural polluters by going directly to the heart of the matter—Wall Street. One such roaring lamb was a small individual investor who lived in Parkersburg, West Virginia. This individual had some modest investments in various mutual funds. His Christian financial adviser worked for an independent broker/dealer called Investment, Management and Research.

During the course of a routine meeting to evaluate the performance of the portfolio, the financial adviser discussed the values represented by the holdings of his mutual fund. The adviser had purchased the values-based screening software from my company and shared the evaluation results with his customer. The software identified the investor's holdings in an IDS stock mutual fund to have a fairly significant percentage of holdings in companies that profited from, or financially supported, abortion.

Once he learned this, the investor became very upset. He asked his adviser to immediately sell the roughly two thousand dollars worth of shares of the fund that he held in his individual retirement account. The adviser reminded him that there was a stiff penalty on his fund for any redemptions.

The investor did not relent. In spite of the fee, he demanded that the adviser sell his fund. The adviser used the software to identify other mutual funds within the same investment category that were culturally clean, yet had equal or better investment performance records. The investor then switched funds to a clean alternative.

In addition, as Senator Bradley encouraged, he sent a letter directly to the IDS fund's money manager in Minneapolis. The letter said, "I am writing to inform you that new information has come to my attention that has led me to avoid investing in your fund. It may surprise you also to learn that this new information has nothing to do with your historical record of investment rate of return, which is actually fairly attractive."

The letter continued, "I am joining a growing national movement of investors that consider the cultural value of the companies represented in their mutual fund to be as important as the investment value they offer. Your portfolio, according to new research that has come to my attention, has a level of ownership in companies that are culturally offensive to me, and that is unacceptable."

The investor sent the letter, expecting no response. The letter made him feel better, and as in most letter-writing campaigns, that was enough. However, within one week of mailing the letter, he received a personal handwritten letter from the billion-dollar money manager. The letter said that the manager had never in his career considered the moral values of the companies he chose to place in his portfolios.

He shared with the investor that he also had strong personal feelings for protecting the lives of the unborn. "Can you give me more information on your data?" he asked. And incredibly, the money manager included his home telephone number in asking for the investor to get back with him.

Understandably, the investor was too intimidated to contact the money manager directly. He passed on the letter to his financial adviser for a recommendation on what to do. They both decided that it would be best to refer it to me since it was my company that delivered the original research. Once I heard of the letter, I immediately called the money manager at IDS in Minneapolis.

In our conversation he told me how appreciative he was that such data existed. While his personal convictions on abortion were strong, he told me that there was no way his parent company, American Express, would ever consider allowing any of its funds to be marketed as "pro-life funds." He thanked me for access to data that would at least allow him to avoid companies involved in the business of abortion in the future.

All three individuals involved in this wonderful story are true roaring lambs among the bulls and bears of Wall Street. Who could have guessed that a small West Virginia investor with two thousand dollars in a billion-dollar fund would make a difference? Who could have guessed that his tenacity and convictions would lead to millions of dollars of stocks being divested? Who knows the millions of dollars of future investment dollars that were subsequently lost by these companies?

Individual investors around the country have far more potential impact than they realize. Christians, especially, tend to underestimate this potential because of the difficulties they have experienced communicating their views in the political arena. In many cases, cynicism has overtaken the passion to write their congressmen, the White House, or even statewide elected officials.

There is a difference in the financial arena, however, and the West Virginia investor stumbled across it. Elected officials are expert in the business of responding to constituent letters. They employ young staffers or interns to separate the vast majority of letters into issue-related stacks. Voters who take the time to write can expect a boilerplate response, ghostwritten by a staffer, and with an authentic-looking signature of the elected representative. In most cases, the closest an elected official gets to your letter is in the final pro or con tally that his or her staff reports.

Wall Street, on the other hand, is not prepared for constituent mail. Mutual fund managers and company investor relations departments are prepared for questions about dividends, payouts, statements, and checks. They are not prepared for well-crafted correspondence from customers who demand accountability for the values that their holdings or companies represent. These letters often go directly to the decision maker you are trying to influence.

As an activist investor, you have the opportunity to extend your influence far more effectively on Wall Street than you can as an activist voter through the White House.

Taking on Other Corporate Activists

There are many other examples of early victory in the culture war on Wall Street. Unfortunately, many political causes that oppose pro-family policies and values in corporate America are better organized, educated, and funded than groups representing Christian faith or values.

Perhaps more effective than other groups are the pro-homosexual groups. Homosexual advocacy groups were very active in covering the case of James Dale, whose application for adult leadership with the Boy Scouts was rejected in 1992. The Boy Scouts told him in writing that homosexuality was contrary to the organization's values.

The Boy Scouts found out that Dale was gay after a newspaper article revealed that he was copresident of Rutgers University's Gay and Lesbian Alliance. The article was about a speech he had given to that group in July 1990. Later that same month, he received a dismissal letter from the Boy Scouts.

Dale decided to sue the Boy Scouts using New Jersey's antidiscrimination act, which bars discrimination based on race, national origin, or sexual orientation. In 1999, the New Jersey Supreme Court held that the Boy Scouts illegally terminated James Dale and were in violation of the antidiscrimination act. The Boy Scouts appealed the case to the United States Supreme Court.

The Supreme Court overturned the lower ruling on June 27, 2000, with a five to four vote stating that the Boy Scouts of America can bar homosexuals from being Scout troop leaders. With this stunning loss, gay and lesbian activists sought new ways to influence the Boy Scouts to change its policy. When the judicial system failed the activists, their next step was directly to Wall Street.

Gay activists identified leading American companies that were financial contributors to the Boy Scouts and began to pressure them publicly to end their support until the Boy Scouts embraced gays as Scout leaders.

In late August 2000, media company Knight Ridder was among the first companies to cave in to the gay pressure. The company asked that the funds it gives nationwide to the United Way not be passed on to the Boy Scouts of America.[2] Other companies joining Knight Ridder were Textron and Merrill Lynch. One company that was reported to have cut off Boy Scouts contributions was Chase Manhattan Bank, although the company only technically announced a "suspension" until the matter was reviewed.

I am editor-in-chief and head of values-based investing at the Christian Internet portal Crosswalk.com. In an editorial for the Crosswalk.com news channel, I wrote, "If you believe that these two companies have lost your trust by their abandonment of the Boy Scouts of America, then they should also lose access to your investment capital. Divest of their company stock, or any mutual funds that hold their stock. Find alternative companies with equally good stock performance that are making choices to build up the integrity of America's children and culture."

I can recognize the pulse of our audience through customer service E-mails we receive. The day after my editorial appeared on the Crosswalk.com site, I began receiving E-mails of support from our audience. Individuals who embraced the roaring-lamb vision decided to take action in their own attempt to make a difference. One reader told me in his E-mail, "I appreciate your column highlighting Chase Manhattan and Merrill Lynch pulling their funding of the Boy Scouts. I have a few brokerage accounts with an affiliate of Chase Manhattan. My accounts have assets of over 1 million dollars and do over $1,000 a month in commissions. I am in the process of writing a letter to these companies and looking to transfer my account because of their recent stand against the Boy Scouts."

Another roaring-lamb investor E-mailed the next day: "In the morning, we will be transferring an IRA of $440,000 from Merrill Lynch and closing a cash account of $27,000 with Chase Manhattan Bank. I cannot wait for them to ask me why!"

I knew that if these were but a sample of viewers who took the time to write to me, hundreds, perhaps thousands, more were transferring money from Chase Manhattan in significant amounts.

One day later, on August 31, Chase Manhattan Bank issued a press release. Chase decided to maintain its funding of the Boy Scouts. The press release said, "Chase has now completed its review and will continue to fund Scout programs. At the end of the day, we do not want to withdraw funding from those programs because doing so would be harmful to thousands of children who benefit significantly from them. We intend to continue working with the Scouts on this evolving issue."

Once again, investors like those who E-mailed me made Chase Manhattan Bank know immediately that there was a financial cost to the company if it chose to advocate the gay and lesbian agenda. Chase officials realized quickly that the cost was too high. They continue to fund the Boy Scouts of America. Pro-family investors won. They beat the gay and lesbian activists in this attempt to intimidate Wall Street.

TAKING ON A CORPORATE GIANT

Perhaps one of the most public cases of standing up to corporate giants involves the international media conglomerate Time Warner. Time Warner's morally challenged music first got national attention with the song "Cop Killer" by rapper artist Ice-T (see chap. 1).

After Ice-T's departure, company President Richard Parsons said only that he "regretted" how the "Cop Killer" issue "was handled." He didn't apologize for ever having been party to the poison it delivered. He was worried only about how it was handled. In a later interview, Parsons said that he was sensitive to harming Time Warner's reputation and that in the future he wanted to be sensitive to any products that might detract from shareholder value. Finally, in a press release, he said that Time Warner, as a company, "ought to have some large responsibility and try to be a force for good."

Time Warner tried to score a public relations victory with letting Ice-T go and by issuing a statement that said all the right words. At the time, there was reason to believe that victory had been won.

In January 1993, Time Warner got a new chairman, Gerald Levin. With Levin leading the company and after the departure of Ice-T, it was difficult to see evidence that Time Warner set out to "be a force for good." Time Warner soon became the largest American distributor of the fringe hard-edged rap music.

It became home to several of the most vulgar performers, such as Tupac Shakur, Dr. Dre, and Snoop Doggy Dog. In fact, the company signed a record deal with a group called Geto Boys after Geffen Records rejected them. Geffen Records, never known for promoting moral standards of any kind, had rejected the deal because of the group's explicit lyrics about mutilating women and having sex with dead bodies.

Geto Boys and "Assassins" were too much for Geffen Records, but they were just fine for Time Warner under Levin's leadership. Levin explained his attitude toward rap and outrageous music in a 1992 opinion piece printed in *USA Today*. He described such violent songs as "Assassins" as a legitimate expression of street culture that deserved an outlet. He also said, "The test of any democratic society lies not in how well it can control expression but in whether it gives the freedom of thought and expression the widest possible latitude, however controversial or exasperating the results may sometimes be. . . . We won't retreat in the face of threats of boycotts or political grandstanding."[3]

This kind of moral bankruptcy at the top of Time Warner motivated a team of cultural warriors to publicly challenge the company. The team was made up of former Secretary of Education William Bennett (and author of the Book of Virtues series) and C. DeLores Tucker, head of the National Political Congress of Black Women. The duo decided to speak at the annual Time Warner shareholder meeting at New York Center. During the meeting, Tucker delivered a seventeen-minute attack on the explicit violence expressed by some of Time Warner's performers. Her speech ended with about one-third of the packed crowd loudly applauding her efforts. Perhaps most importantly, one person applauding her comments was on the Time Warner board. It wasn't just any board member either. It was Henry Luce III, the son of *Time*'s founder.

After the public shareholder meeting, Time Warner executives agreed to meet privately with Tucker and Bennett in Levin's office at the Time Warner Manhattan headquarters. Included in the meetings was Michael Fuchs, who had just been appointed to head the music division after years of leading Time Warner's Home Box Office (HBO) division.

Both Fuchs and Levin were testy to Bennett and Tucker as the meeting began. It started with Tucker asking the Time Warner executives to simply read aloud the lyrics of the song "Big Man with a Gun" by Time Warner artist Nine Inch Nails. The song describes putting a pistol to a woman's head and forcing her to perform oral sex. Tucker also asked them to read from the Geto Boys' song "Mind of a Lunatic," which is a melody of rape and murder.

Levin and Fuchs declined. Their response was simply, "Well, this is the authentic voice of the black community."

Tucker angrily responded, "It is not the authentic voice of the black community to refer to its women as b——, whores, and sluts." Bennett later said that Tucker was so angry, he thought she was going to go across the table and grab Levin.[4]

Fuchs and Levin had no response. Tucker angrily walked out of the meeting for a short time and then returned. Bennett continued the discussion. He asked, "What social good does this do? What good at all does this do?"

Levin responded, "This is free expression."

"Yeah, we know it's free expression," Bennett replied. "Why are you cashing in on it? And is it the right thing to do?" Later, in his not-so-subtle manner, Bennett asked Levin and Fuchs, "Are you folks morally disabled?"

He received what he considered to be a patronizing and predictable reply. Levin said, "What is art? Art is hard to interpret. Who's to decide what is pornography and what isn't?"

"Forget the freshman seminar in philosophy," Bennett retorted. "Why are you guys trying to light this fire? It's not as if we have too little violence in America. It's not as if we have too little violence against women in America. You don't need to be lighting this kindling and letting this fire burn."

Levin disagreed. "No, these lyrics are not necessarily bad for children to listen to." He added, "Elvis was more controversial in his day than some rap lyrics are today."

"Is there any stuff so bad, any message so vile, so stupid, so counterproductive, so hurtful to people, to Americans, to children, and to families that you people will not sell if you can make a profit?" asked Bennett.

In the aftermath of the meeting, Fuchs charged Bennett with seeking confrontation and publicity. "He came in with no information and no credentials to discuss any of this intelligently. I guess he thought he was the self-appointed marshal riding in on a white horse to be the arbiter of morals."[5]

Bennett later reflected, "I was impressed with the lack of candor. It was extremely pompous. Here were these guys in $4,000 suits making us feel like we were lucky to be getting the time of day." He added that the mood of the meeting was more contentious than any meeting he had been in, even while he was the national drug czar or as Secretary of Education.[6]

With Bennett's leadership, public pressure began to grow slowly on Time Warner. Newspapers around the country began to weigh in on the story. Syndicated columnist Don Feder commented, "Its ears crammed with cash, the entertainment industry is stone deaf. The lives of children, the safety of women, the survival of our society mean nothing next to the profits of movie studios and record companies."[7]

Senator Bob Dole took Bennett's lead and turned up the public pressure on Time Warner. On the evening of May 31, 1995, Senator Dole publicly targeted Time Warner in a speech he gave in Los Angeles.

> There is a difference between the description of evil through art and the marketing of evil through commerce, and I would ask the executives at Time Warner a question. Is this what you intend to accomplish with your careers? Must you debase our nation and threaten our children for the sake of corporate profits? . . .Let me be specific. One of the companies on the leading edge of coarseness and violence is Time Warner. It is a symbol of how much we have lost. In the 1930s its corporate predecessor, Warner Brothers, made a series of movies including _G-Men_ for the purpose of restoring dignity and public confidence in police. It made movies to help the war effort in the early 1940s. Its company slogan, put on a billboard across from the studio was "Combining Good Citizenship with Good Picture Making."[8]

Today Time Warner owns a company called Interscope Records, which columnist John Leo called the "cultural equivalent of owning half the world's mustard gas factories. . . . I cannot bring myself to repeat the lyrics of some of the music Time Warner promotes. But our children do. . . . The corporate executives who dismiss my criticism should not misunderstand. Mine is not the objection of some tiny group of zealots or an ideological fringe. From inner-city mothers to suburban mothers to families in rural America, parents are afraid and growing angry. There was once a time when parents felt the community of adults was on their side. Now they feel surrounded by forces assaulting their children and their code of ethics."[9]

Time Warner began to realize that something had to be done. Even though the company earned $85 million from the sales of rap music in 1994,[10] there was obvious concern that the controversy could spill over to hurt sales of other company products or reduce investor interest in purchasing its stock. While the fifteen members of Time Warner's board of directors were generally supportive of Gerald Levin, cracks were beginning to show after Dole's public attack. Company insiders said that several of them internally echoed the concerns of William Bennett and Robert Dole. The leaders of the group were Henry Luce (son of *Time*'s founder), former U.S. Trade representative Carla Hills, and former commissioner of Major League Baseball Fay Vincent.[11] In fact, Luce said in an interview, "Some of us have known for many, many years that the freedoms under the First Amendment are not totally unlimited. I think it is perhaps the case that some people associated with the company have belatedly come to realize this."[12]

On September 27, 1995, Time Warner capitulated to the public pressure and announced its sale of 50 percent of Interscope Records (and its subsidiary Death Row Records). Michael Fuchs's public statement on the day of its sale said, "This decision is not about any particular kind of music." Rather, "the nature of our agreement with Interscope precluded us from any meaningful involvement or discussion regarding Interscope's music." Fuchs was referring to an unsuccessful effort that Time Warner had made in August 1995 to review all new material from Interscope and Death Row Records for objectionable material before being released. Interscope flatly refused. Time Warner had no other choice but to sell it.[13]

The shareholders and the culture at large won. They beat the largest and most powerful entertainment company in the world. There was no apparent change of moral conviction in the heart of Time Warner's leader Gerald Levin. But Time Warner certainly recognized a financial cost that it was not willing to bear in order to keep Interscope and Death Row Records. The cost was too high, so it sold the record labels.

Sure, I would prefer for the company to make the same decision because the hearts of the Time Warner executives were changed. And that still may happen. Yet the right decisions were still made by Time Warner for less-than-perfect reasons: purely economic. People of faith in America can influence corporate America to make the right choices for economic reasons.

Importantly, it is significant to understand that in each of the cases of victory that have been demonstrated, the actual flow of hundreds of millions of dollars out of any of the companies involved never had to actually take place in order for the companies to be influenced. The key to success for individual investors to win in the culture war on Wall Street is simply perception.

If company leadership can get a glimpse of the financial cost that could take place if people of faith across the country joined in a withdrawal of investment capital from their firms, then there is sufficient influence at that time to lead a company to abandon policies and products that pollute our culture. This fact dramatically empowers Christian investors. Unlike the political arena in which votes are counted to determine policies, company leaders will base decisions about their policies and products on trends and feedback that impact the bottom line—their stock price, profit, and capitalization.

Victory over Pornography

Frequent travelers like myself have the luxury of good quality hotel properties to choose from these days. The hospitality industry has grown substantially in the numbers of guestrooms available through the decade of the '90s. Hotels like Marriott's Courtyard chain were specifically designed with the business traveler in mind. As I have especially learned over the past few years, business travel is difficult enough, but it helps to have my choice of hotels with convenient locations and dependable quality.

The same holds true for families. Today families can expect to find "all suite" motels (available in nearly every metropolitan area) that offer many family amenities such as two televisions, beds in separate rooms, and a kitchenette. Many hotels, such as Embassy Suites, advertise their benefits directly to family travelers.

Ironically, the choice to not have hard-core pornography available in your room has dramatically declined. Years ago, very few hotels had sophisticated pay-per-view TV services that provided "adult" programming in the rooms. Today, hard-core pornography is almost universally available, regardless of the hotel chain you select. The last available figures I could find showed that more than $175 million was spent on in-room hard-core pornography at American hotels in 1996.[14]

The reason so many hotels offer pornography boils down to money. Large hotel chains rely on companies that will provide all of the televisions in their hotels for free if the hotel agrees to hook up the pay-per-view systems these companies provide. The hotels then share in the revenue of all of the movies that are selected. The pornography being sold is not R-rated movies filled with seminudity and sexual innuendo. Rather, it's hard-core and extreme—X-rated movies with graphic sex.

Imagine the savings by not having to pay for any televisions in an eight-hundred-room hotel? Imagine your corporate treasurer deciding between these two options: (1) using company cash to purchase new televisions for each of the rooms that provide no ongoing revenue, or (2) using someone else's cash to buy the televisions and then using the televisions to provide future cash flow?

Admittedly, it is a very powerful temptation for anyone. Moral relativism often accompanies any discussion of this as well. A Marriott spokesman reminded me that Marriott doesn't force anyone to watch the pornography. "In fact," he said, "a guest has to push the select button twice before it activates the movie." Other hotels boast that a family can call the front desk and ask that the adult movie programming be disabled so that children cannot access it without their parents' knowledge.

These options sound good, but they both represent caving in to the spread of moral poison for the benefit of profit. I was told by a hotel official that some of the highest percentage of adult movie selections occurred when a Promise Keepers convention was in his town. I'm sure this was an unfair attack, but I'm also certain that thousands of the men at a Promise Keepers conference could be tempted to watch pornography in the privacy of their hotel rooms.

I doubt that very few, if any, of those men at a Promise Keepers convention hired a prostitute to come to their room for sexual pleasure. However, I am certain that if Marriott provided a pay-per-prostitute to sit in everyone's room at night, only to be used by the choice of the hotel guest in the privacy of his own room, the number of sexual encounters with prostitutes would significantly increase. The Scriptures are clear that we are not to place ourselves in areas of temptations. We are all sinners living in a fallen world. Hiding moral decisions behind the relativism argument of "personal choice" is meaningless. Hotel chains face a clear responsibility for making pornography conveniently available to hotel guests.

One company has said yes to bypassing some profit and no to pornography—Omni Hotels, a private chain of more than forty luxury hotels across Canada, the United States, and Mexico. The company is wholly owned and operated by TRT Holdings of Dallas, Texas.

In November 1999, the company announced that it was removing all pornography from its hotels. The decision to drop the service was first made by Omni owner Robert Rowling. Shortly after buying the company, Rowling was staying at an Omni hotel and noticed the pornography in the room. There were also "adult" magazines in the hotel gift shops. Rowling asked his partners, "Should we really be profiting from pornography?"[15]

It was easy to take the pornographic magazines out of the gift shops, but removing the movies was more difficult. Omni wanted to substitute a movie service that would provide access to first-rate movies without the porn. Every single company Omni contacted would offer the service only if pornography was included.

Eventually, one of the leaders in the business, LodgeNet Corporation, told Rowlings that it would develop a package that fit Omni's needs. The movie service Omni had been using immediately came to the hotels and removed the televisions it had provided for free in exchange for offering pornographic movies. Rowlings estimated that the cost to the company for replacing the televisions was initially at least $4 million. Omni will also lose any revenue it would have received from customers signing up for the pay-per-view movies.

In a letter from Rowlings to a Crosswalk.com representative, Rowlings simply stated his reasoning for the decision: "It is the right thing to do." I take my hat off to Robert Rowlings for choosing to do business in a way that uplifts our families and our culture, even at the cost of losing additional profits.

VICTORIES FOR THE UNBORN

Planned Parenthood, the nation's leader in promoting abortion, has a long history of attracting corporate contributions from public companies in order to subsidize its services. According to public records, he organization has received more than $5 million per year from corporate gifts. These gifts come from the profits of public companies, to be used as the company leadership sees appropriate.

More and more, company shareholders are becoming vocal about their opposition to this practice. Why should corporate management use the shareholders' money to fund groups as controversial as Planned Parenthood when thousands of other nonprofit groups that do not carry the same moral and political baggage compete for the same money? There are thousands of organizations designed to help the needy and less fortunate, designed to uplift society and not destroy life, that are not political hot potatoes. Why shouldn't management be challenged when it chooses to send money to Planned Parenthood?

A *Business Week* article in 1990 was titled "Planned Parenthood Didn't Plan On This." The article detailed how some corporate leaders came under fire for supporting the abortion industry. "Inundated by letters and calls from vocal, well-organized abortion foes, several companies have cut off contributions to Planned Parenthood." One corporate leader was quoted as saying, "No CEO is comfortable with letters saying 'You're murdering babies.'"[16]

In March 1990, pro-life activists claimed a major victory when corporate giant AT&T announced it was ending its twenty-five-year tradition of sending an annual fifty-thousand-dollar contribution to Planned Parenthood. Planned Parenthood responded by placing full-page advertisements in several of the nation's most prominent newspapers. The ads said, "Caving In to Extremists, AT&T Hangs Up on Planned Parenthood." The ads also referred to those at AT&T and others who opposed Planned Parenthood as a "close-minded, intolerant" minority.

In spite of the public attacks from pro-abortion activists, leaders at AT&T recognized that costs associated with continued support of Planned Parenthood would be higher than they were willing to assume.

Planned Parenthood recently lost another corporate donor in General Mills. During the 1998 annual shareholders meeting of the giant food manufacturer, many shareholders attended in culmination of a protest over the corporation's tradition of sending money to Planned Parenthood. Charles Kleinbrook and his mother spoke to the General Mills board at the meeting. "You should be concerned with feeding children, not killing them," said Mrs. Kleinbrook. Eric Larson, with the office of Investor Relations at General Mills, said the company had received "thousands of letters" in opposition to the donations.[17]

The resolution to end the donations was voted down at the board meeting. However, within the following month, a majority of the General Mills board of directors did vote to end future contributions to Planned Parenthood.

One more success story involves the German pharmaceutical giant Hoechst AG. Hoechst was the parent company of the producer of the abortion pill RU-486, known chemically as mifepristone. Since 1988 the pill has been legally available in France, where it was originally created.

At first, Hoechst tried to avoid the political and social backlash from producing the drug by announcing that it would not produce the drug for distribution in the United States. The company even gave away the rights for distribution and production of the drug to the pro-abortion Population Council for free. (The Population Council is a nonprofit agency based in New York.)

The council thought the move was a victory so that it could take the lead in identifying an appropriate manufacturer and distributor for RU-486 since Hoechst had been unwilling to do so. Hoechst thought the move was a victory because it believed that as long as it wasn't involved in making or distributing the drug in the United States, it would avoid further social disruption.

This was not the case because of the efforts of pro-life activists to keep both organizations accountable. Finally, Hoechst sold off all rights for distribution and production of RU-486 because it found that the costs were too high. Meanwhile, back in the United States, the stealth-funded Population Council was successful through the Clinton administration in getting selected Planned Parenthood Clinics to distribute RU-486.

Hemant Shah, a pharmaceutical industry analyst, offered her thoughts on why RU-486 has never made it into commercial production in the United States. "The question is whether the financial gain is worth the political headache. And for most pharmaceutical companies, the answer is no."[18] I am certain that any financial analyst would agree that the only reason "political headaches" bother companies is because of the resulting financial fallout on the bottom line. Once again, where legislation and public debates have failed to gain much ground in the fight over abortion, focusing on companies that profit from it has been very successful.

There is one common message in these various stories of success: Roaring lambs _can_ beat the bulls and bears of Wall Street.

CHAPTER 11

BULLS, BEARS, AND LAMBS— EVALUATING A WINNING FORMULA FOR CHRISTIANS ON WALL STREET

Christians are not responsible for the choices others make. We are, however, personally and individually responsible when we have not given those within our spheres of influence a clear cut Christian alternative as they make important choices in life.
BOB BRINER,
Final Roar

ACTIVISM ON WALL STREET to pursue social or cultural change is not a new idea. Political leaders, leaders of social causes and advocacy groups, and even some Christian ministries have attempted in the past to effect a lasting impact on our culture by using the influence of Wall Street. From boycotts and shareholder resolutions to letter-writing campaigns, there have been various experiences of success and failure.

Values-based investing is not the only solution. To uplift our culture and impact corporate America as roaring lambs, we need to familiarize ourselves with many pieces of the puzzle. Many other strategies can be used to supplement values-based investing in today's culture war on Wall Street. Many of these other strategies have been mentioned or referred to in other areas of this book.

How should Christians and people of faith engage Wall Street? What tools in addition to values-based investing are available? What are the experiences of others who have engaged in these strategies? Perhaps most importantly, just how do these corporate activist strategies fit with the message of the gospel that we are ultimately responsible to promote?

EPS—EVALUATING STRATEGIES TO SUPPLEMENT VALUES-BASED INVESTING ON WALL STREET

EPS usually stands for earnings per share when it comes to evaluating companies on Wall Street. However, I am using EPS in this context to stand for effectiveness, practicality, and spiritual cost. I have completed a report card evaluation of the many tactics that can supplement VBI. The scores are designed to evaluate each investment strategy for the following three factors.

1. Effectiveness—When successful, some strategies may actually lead to a change in the corporation involved so that anti-family or offensive products and policies are changed. In other words, how likely is it that the company will actually change in the way you are trying to influence it to change?

2. Practicality—While a certain strategy may work extremely well, just how likely is it that Christians and people of faith can actually succeed in accomplishing the strategy? If it isn't a realistic goal, it may not be worth promoting, no matter how effective it might be.

3. Spiritual Cost—We have a responsibility to do more than simply count the score at the end of the battle. Christians, like anyone else, can get caught up in an "end justifies the means" attitude. We must guard against using a strategy that would stain the glory and potential witness of the gospel. Corporate tactics in the name of promoting morality can become an end in themselves. A tactic can also become an impediment to more effective communication of the gospel to our society. This, of course, is counterproductive to the extreme, because in the final analysis, the only way to protect our culture ultimately is by changing hearts.

Also, cost is measured traditionally in dollars. A measure of the spiritual cost must be an examination of the money and resources needed to complete the strategy. If a great deal of money must be raised from donations and therefore taken away from other worthwhile ministries and causes, then the strategy may have a ministerial opportunity cost. Using money to execute a strategy may effectively take money out of the pockets of other ministries.

With these factors in mind, let's evaluate several strategies.

COMPANY TAKEOVERS

Corporate takeovers are perhaps the most effective way to influence change in a public company. It is obvious that if you gain control over the management of a company by purchasing a controlling interest, you then can change the policies and products any way you choose. The problem with this strategy is the price tag. Who has the hundreds of millions of dollars, sometimes billions of dollars, needed to buy enough stock to control a company? This is a simple, straightforward idea. It is also a fairly unrealistic one.

Perhaps the best chance this strategy ever had of working for social conservatives began in 1984. Just after the reelection of President Ronald Reagan in November 1984, conservatives were healing from another bruising campaign season. Once again, political conservatives were tiring of what they saw as an overwhelming liberal bias in the mainstream media. Rush Limbaugh and political talk radio had not yet impacted the national scene, and certainly the networks still had a grip on controlling the nation's news. The Internet was not around to provide alternate views.

At the same time, Republicans as a whole, and social conservative activists in particular, were celebrating a huge mandate from the electorate based on Reagan's landslide victory. Political strategists behind the scenes were searching for new ways to deal with the liberal media. The leading direct-mail fund-raiser for conservatives, Richard Viguerie, had an idea. He felt that in order to accomplish the conservatives' political goals for the next four years, there had to be a change in the media. Viguerie organized a group of conservatives and hired Wall Street specialists to implement a bold new strategy. The strategy was to find prospective print and television media targets they could buy or take financial control of. The idea was to bring together enough conservative investors from around the country and pool their money in order to take financial control of targeted public companies.

Within a week of Reagan's election victory, a man named Thomas Ellis decided to move ahead in a plan to develop a strategy to take over CBS. The network and featured news anchor Dan Rather were a political nemeses to social conservatives. The plan was to rally social conservatives from around the country to buy CBS, gain control of the company through the financial markets, and ultimately change the news coverage to a friendly tone for Republicans.

On November 13, Ellis and two other North Carolina lawyers, Carter Wrenn and James Cain, officially formed a group called Fairness in Media. All three organizers had close political ties with North Carolina senator Jesse Helms. Wrenn and Ellis were both affiliated with the National Congressional Club, a conservative political action committee.

On January 10, 1985, Fairness in Media organizers filed the necessary papers with the Securities and Exchange Commission, disclosing that it intended to buy a controlling interest in CBS. Senator Helms helped finance an initial $500,000 to pay for the mailing of nearly 1 million letters. The letters, signed by Helms, asked conservatives to

each purchase twenty shares of CBS stock. To gain an absolute majority, the group would have to collectively pool more than $1.5 billion
in purchases of CBS stock. Wall Street analysts were doubtful of the
takeover prospects.

Fairness in Media organizers also began conducting discussions
with third parties, seeking more money and capital in their bid to buy
CBS. The mantra supporting the campaign around the country was
"Become Dan Rather's Boss."

How did the campaign end? What was the conclusion? It is obvious that CBS remains intact, and Dan Rather still has his job. Despite
these well-organized efforts at a time of unprecedented power for political conservatives, Fairness in Media failed in every measurement.
Anyone who would have acted on the call to buy twenty shares of CBS
stock on January 10, 1985, would have paid $1,450 in total, or $72.50
per share. By March 29, 1985, the price of the stock had gone up
51 percent to $109.75 per share.[1]

The many lawsuits filed against Fairness in Media included one by
CBS that charged that Fairness in Media was "attempting to manipulate the market in CBS stock through statements intended to create the
false impression that FIM's efforts will result in a tender offer or other
conventional takeover of CBS."[2]

Ironically, conservatives did nothing to effectively change CBS. In
fact, a report card on the effort can conclude the following:

- The very people the organizers were trying to get out of power
  were ultimately more in control than before. In fact, the owners
  of CBS were actually rewarded by a 51 percent windfall profit as
  a result of the conservatives' efforts. The cumulative new buying
  pressure on the stock created by the stock purchase campaign
  moved the market and pushed the stock up. The speculation in
  the marketplace of putting CBS in play for a takeover also led to
  increased buying to further drive the price of the stock up.

- Millions of dollars and thousands of hours of resources were wasted in the failed effort. Consider what positive and uplifting campaigns this same money and time could have been used for.
- The witness of these efforts was a disaster. Conservatives and Christians involved in the campaign were seen to be hateful and revengeful. For Christians who participated, their credibility and opportunity to present the gospel in this context was destroyed.

Although the strategy of direct company control would seem to be the best of all possible worlds, it is evident from this example that it is all but impossible to actually acquire all of the offensive companies on the public market for the purposes of cleaning up their policies and products. I submit that this strategy also spawns a lot of collateral damage in the big picture of promoting the values of Christ at the same time that we are fighting for our values. As mentioned, the strategy of engaging a company in a hostile takeover does very little to promote a witness for God in the meantime. In the final analysis, the corporate takeover strategy is the most difficult and leaves the greatest damage along the way.

Report Card for Company Takeovers
Effectiveness: A+
Practicality: F
Spiritual Cost: F

CORPORATE GOVERNANCE MOVEMENT

T. Boone Pickens is considered by many to be the father of the movement that tries to make company leaders and boards of directors accountable to the real owners: the shareholders. Traditionally classified as a corporate raider, he would mount hostile takeover bids for companies that he felt were not being managed to maximize shareholder value.

In the corporate governance movement, the overall goal is to force company leaders to be more frugal with their money, reduce executive compensation, and increase the company stock price for the shareholders. The strategy of choice is the shareholder resolution.

Shareholder resolutions allow activists to have an advisory vote among the shareholders regarding their cause at a company's annual shareholders' meeting. While the vote is only advisory in nature, activists point out that the negative publicity that such a public discussion and debate may lead to can be very influential. For example, a company may discontinue a negative environmental practice rather than have it brought up for debate at the shareholders' meeting.

Most resolutions, however, end up having no quantifiable impact. Even if a resolution receives a majority of votes, it remains only an advisory vote to the company's board of directors. Pickens complained that shareholder resolutions still don't have the teeth that he feels they should have. "I buy the stock. I'm part owner, and you let me make an advisory vote? That's a silly d—- way to run your business," he said.[3]

Some companies, such as Disney and Maxxam, have been accused of holding their annual meetings in exotic locations specifically to make it harder for many shareholders to attend, thereby diminishing their power. The Securities and Exchange Commission continues to weigh in with new regulations that make it even more difficult for shareholder resolutions to be effective. Ultimately, the shareholder resolution is more about feeling good about trying to make a change rather than actually about influencing a change in the targeted company.

Other more aggressive tactics in the corporate governance movement can be effective but are certainly more rare. For example, a group known as Institutional Shareholder Services was trying to influence Sears to improve its earnings and enhance the stock price. Rather than relying on shareholder resolutions, the organization took out full-page ads in the *Wall Street Journal* that called the directors of Sears, Roebuck and Company "nonperforming assets." That ad did prompt the Sears directors to divest several unrelated divisions that were dragging earnings down.[4]

In the end, even some of the top leaders of the corporate governance movement are losing faith. Sarah Teslik, head of the Council of Institutional Investors, has been fighting to influence corporate boards since 1985 through shareholder resolutions and internal dialogue as shareholders. "But we have gotten ourselves in a position to do something that is absolutely pointless. . . . Their answer is, essentially, 'We are the company. You are not.'" Teslik summarizes her evaluation, "We are seriously thinking about closing shop because we may be wasting money."[5]

Report Card for the Corporate Governance Movement

Effectiveness: F

Practicality: C

Spiritual Cost: C

CONSUMER BOYCOTTS

What do Home Depot, Gap, Shell Oil, Texaco, CBS, Eastman Kodak, Metallica, the NBA, California grapes, Washington Mutual Bank, and Intel all have in common? They are all being actively targeted by organized consumer boycotts. The reasons behind boycott efforts are extremely diverse. There are even groups designed to boycott the boycotters.

Strategically, boycotts are designed to scare companies or organizations into changing their policies out of fear that the boycotts will lead to lower revenues. Philosophically, boycotts are designed to use the pooled financial resources of consumers as a weapon of leverage for social or political change. At this level there are some similarities between boycotts and values-based investing.

However, the similarities end there. The truth of boycotts is that it remains tremendously difficult to organize enough individuals, each spending a few dollars, to collectively make any significant impact, or even any perceived impact, on a company. In a world in which families are searching for new ways to save time and add convenience in an increasingly hectic schedule, boycotts rely on consumers to take the time to comb through "boycott product lists" while in the grocery store. In general, the effort required for practical execution of a consumer boycott is far more than anyone other than committed activists will accept.

Of course, the most recognizable boycott campaign for Christians is the Disney boycott. Personally, I agree that there are many legitimate reasons to want to avoid encouraging Disney by not buying its products. I have been in many radio and television debates over Disney policies myself. However, even working in a Christian company and working with national ministries every week, I have not met one single person who has made a diligent commitment to honor the Disney boycott with his or her personal buying decisions.

Let me explain how complicated the relatively simple Disney boycott can be for a family. To effectively keep any consumer dollars from flowing to Disney, you would have to avoid all of the following: Walt Disney World; Disneyland; EuroDisney; Tokyo Disney; Walt Disney-branded products (such as educational products, toys, plates, cups, clothes, hats, music, costumes, books, cassette tapes, trinkets, etc.); Buena Vista-branded home videos, movies, and television; ABC television shows, movies, news, and sports programs; Touchstone Pictures movies; Hollywood Pictures movies; Caravan Pictures movies; Miramax Films movies; A&E cable television network; the Disney cable channel; ESPN, ESPN2, ESPN News, or ESPN Classic cable channels; Lifetime Television cable network; music from Hollywood Records; books published by Disney Publishing, Hyperion Press, or

Chilton Publications; Disney-owned stores in malls across America; and watching the Anaheim Mighty Ducks hockey team.

It's not as easy as it looks, even for the Disney boycott. One of the worst enemies of boycotts is common sense. Corporate boards understand that boycotts are very rarely effective. The most a boycott can usually hope for is to catch the interest of the mainstream press in order to add free negative publicity. The impact then becomes the negative publicity rather than the boycott itself.

Nike is a good example. There is an organized boycott against Nike because of alleged hiring of underage workers for poverty-level wages in Third World countries. In evaluating the impact of the boycott, there is no evidence that company earnings or revenues have been reduced by the boycotts. Just watch any sporting event on television, and you will see that nearly every sports uniform known to humankind has the famous Nike "swoosh" logo on it. In fact, even Chinese athletes at the 2000 Sydney Olympics wore the Nike logo. The only reason that Nike has publicly responded to this boycott is the national media attention it has received, not because of any recognized dip in product purchases.

Sometimes consumer boycotts have a way of actually working against the agenda that it is trying to advance. A case in point is the American Family Association (AFA). Don Wildmon, AFA's leader, stood firm in his boycott stance against Disney when its television subsidiary, ABC, released a special animated show on the parables of Jesus called "The Miracle Maker." The program was to be aired around Easter 2000. The program, unlike the miniseries "Noah," received wide acclaim from Christians as well as the entertainment industry. There was even a movement among Southern Baptists requesting an exemption from the endorsed Disney boycott so they could watch "The Miracle Maker" in good conscience.

Wildmon released a statement that said no matter how good the gospel message was in "The Miracle Maker," he called on Christians to boycott it. After it aired, there was almost unanimous endorsement of the theological integrity of the show and the effectiveness of getting the message of Jesus Christ to people through the show. In England, the Bible Society used the show in a campaign to reach 1 million people "so that they can experience the story and the understanding of the Gospel story."[6]

In this instance, Wildmon and those who supported his stance stood on the ground of self-determined policy even though it stood in the way of Christianity's ultimate mission of communicating the gospel of Christ. When boycotts close the doors of the gospel, they are counterproductive.

In the final analysis, boycotts are not meaningless. They do offer an opportunity to create dialogue and public recognition of a company's faults. This is certainly valuable. Clearly, boycotts have a place within a broader strategy that utilizes other tactics as well.

Ultimately, however, boycotts deal much more with feelings than results. It makes an activist feel good to bypass a product to support his personal opinions and values. I do this often myself and experience that same good feeling. But feelings don't change policy. Feelings can trap a person into the illogical rationalization that he or she is making a difference. When it comes to company policy, boycotts by themselves do not scare or intimidate large corporations. Without any fear, there is no change.

Report Card for Consumer Boycotts

Effectiveness: F

Practicality: F

Spiritual Cost: D

SPIRITUAL INVESTING

A hybrid of socially responsible investing principles and "spiritual values," the philosophy of "spiritual investing" has both promise and drawbacks. This philosophy was pioneered by legendary money manager Sir John Templeton. Templeton created one of the most successful and largest mutual fund companies in the world, now based in Nassau, Bahamas.

At the heart of the philosophy is a consideration of what social good your investments will have in addition to the traditional financial return you expect, much like traditional socially responsible investing. Templeton's theory was to invest in stocks when they were out of favor and severely undervalued. He called it investing at the "point of maximum pessimism." A strategy that some on Wall Street call "bottom fishing," the philosophy has proven to work well for patient investors who do their financial homework to select the right value situations. Templeton also recognized that people living in economically depressed areas (hence, where companies are doing poorly and are "out of favor" with investors) are also those most in need of investment capital to help pull themselves out of economic despair.

Templeton said this about his philosophy: "We always felt that we were doing good—not only for our investors, helping them to make profits, but also for the nations where we invested. If we send money to buy shares in corporations in the poverty stricken nations, then those corporations can expand more readily and help people. Furthermore, most of those poor nations need infrastructure, such as more pure water, or more telephones, or more highways, and you can't do that by local savings. So you need to have the foreigners come in and buy shares in order that your infrastructure can be the foundation of the entrepreneurship among the local people."[7]

Templeton's corollary has worked well with investment performance when measured over the years. Certainly, the investments he made in companies that operate in poor nations have benefited the economies and the citizens of those countries. In the same way, spiritual investing encourages investments in community development banks that make loans to those in poverty who would not qualify for loans through traditional banks or financial institutions.

Like socially responsible investing (SRI), spiritual investing focuses on what social good your money can do while you also make a prudent financial gain. The difference is a third aspect to this social good. What SRI promotes as the double bottom line—social good plus financial gain—spiritual investing promotes as the "triple bottom line." This adds a "spiritual enrichment" to social good and personal financial gain.

"This higher dimension keeps wealth managers connected to the gracious Creative Spirit, and therefore to the souls of we the Created, and is common to many spiritual traditions" said Gary Moore, a leading disciple of spiritual investing. Moore's philosophy is "not just avoiding harm but doing good." He said that the spiritual dimension of investing to help the poor leads to personal joy. "The joy I've often seen in the face of Sir John (Templeton) . . . is not unlike that often seen in the face of the Dalai Lama. I believe that joy affirms that triple rewards are not only possible for investors, but that they are complementary."

Spiritual investing further clarifies a difference and a middle ground between the social-good-only aspects of SRI and the Christian-based avoidance discipline of values-based investing. Moore explains this distinction by quoting the Dalai Lama: "'An ethical act is one where we refrain from causing harm to others' experience or expectation of happiness. Spiritual acts we can describe in terms of those qualities such as love, compassion, patience, forgiveness, humility, tolerance, and so on which presume some level of concern for others' well-being.'"[8]

Spiritual investing has an undeniably positive impact on people's lives, much like worldwide relief agencies such as World Vision and Compassion International. But unlike World Vision's and Compassion's beliefs, spiritual investing's underlying theology and spiritual foundation are wide-ranging. Foundations of the Jewish faith, Hinduism, Christianity, and Eastern religions seem to be equally spread across its theology. Spiritual investing helps people much like a United Nations social services program helps people. Poverty is relieved and hope is restored, but the central message of the gospel is absent.

Report Card for Spiritual Investing
Effectiveness: B
Practicality: B
Spiritual Cost: D

COMPARISONS WITH VALUES-BASED INVESTING

Values-based investing represents a fundamental methodology to strip away exposure to and promotion of businesses whose policies are antithetical to the Word of God as expressed through the Bible. As an avoidance investing strategy, it does not seek to define social good or justice but empowers individual people of faith to purge evil out of their portfolios. Collectively, this leads to positively influencing the culture around us so that the gospel message has more freedom to be spread and heard.

Yet there are some specific issues of comparison and distinction that should be reviewed further between values-based investing and the other investment activities that have been reviewed previously.

First, several key distinctions between values-based investing and boycotts are often misunderstood. Both are designed to leverage the influence of money in order to change company products or policies. One distinction, as explained earlier, is the tremendous leverage advantage that investors have over individual consumers.

For example, to lead to a reduction in sales to Disney of $100 million you have to organize 10 million individual consumers to not purchase a $10 Disney video. On the other hand, to lead to the sale of

$100 million of Disney stock on the open market, you only have to convince a handful of money managers who have decision-making control over that many shares of Disney stock. It takes far fewer resources and far less effort to achieve a more effective impact on the company you are trying to influence.

Second, there is a key distinction between the responsibilities and effectiveness of consumer activism and activism revolving around ownership. There is a difference between the scriptural and ethical responsibility of buying a product associated with a company and actually being a part-owner of a company. As a shareholder of a company, you are an owner of the company and you earn profits from all areas of the company. For example, as a Disney shareholder, you can't ask to earn profits only from the Disney films division and exclude profits from the Miramax films division. Your investment capital is invested into the company, and the board of directors is elected by and ultimately responsible to you and the other shareholders. There is no one to pass the buck to as a shareholder. The policies and products of the company reflect on the owners, or shareholders, of the company.

There is far more flexibility in choosing what to support with consumer dollars. For example, how much does it support the movie *Priest* (distributed by Disney subsidiary Miramax) when you buy a *101 Dalmatians* video for your daughter? Aren't you specifically supporting a product you wish Disney would recognize they need more of?

I know that many people feel, out of principle, that they want nothing to do with any product of Disney. That's fine. But what you must also understand is that your decision really has nothing to do with influencing the company to change. Your decision is a personal one that allows you to live by your own principles, thereby causing you to feel better about your consumer spending decisions.

Once, I was interviewed in a financial magazine called *Ticker* concerning the philosophy of values-based investing. The lead sentence in the article said, "There's no reason to look for Scott Fehrenbacher at Walt Disney World anytime soon." The problem was that the article was published just one day before I took my entire family to Orlando for a family vacation that included Disney World. The article and the reporter didn't grasp the difference between the responsibility of stock ownership versus the limited value or responsibility of consumer purchases. I did not take my family to Disney's *Priest.* I took my children to ride "It's a Small World" and the "Tea Cups."

If we are to be roaring-lamb investors, then our actions must speak as loudly as our words. Our actions must mean more than political spin. There is a great difference between supporting family-friendly Disney products through my purchases while denying anti-family products access to my money, versus joining Michael Eisner as an owner of Disney and profiting from both family-friendly and anti-family products as a shareholder.

While I do not condemn consumer boycotts, it is important to recognize the important distinctions between the principle of consumer activism and the obedience of values-based investing.

A TAPESTRY OF OBEDIENCE

These individual plans and strategies for managing your investment dollars come down to a matter of a means rather than an end. It is too easy to get wrapped up into such strategies as a belief that any of them, or any combination of them, will heal the wrongs of this world. They won't.

However, we have been commanded by Christ to live obediently. Integrating the morality, the truth, and the love of Christ into our everyday lives continues to be the challenge faced by Christians. One of the areas most often overlooked in this search for obedience is the use of the financial resources with which God has blessed us. Christians have spent a great deal of effort and resources over the past decades searching for answers to integrating the Christian walk into daily political and cultural discourse, but extraordinarily little has centered on how to integrate the Christian walk with financial assets.

None of the complementary options to values-based investing identified in this chapter are perfect solutions. It is clear that some options have greater convenience or effectiveness than others. Our challenge as investors seeking to be obedient, seeking to live out the worldview we have with the influence of our financial assets, is to personally choose a mixture of solutions that work for our own personal circumstances. Using an underlying values-based investing philosophy, we can choose complementary strategies that, woven together, form our own personal tapestry of financial obedience.

CHAPTER 12

A CHRISTIAN WORLDVIEW IN A POST-CHRISTIAN WORLD

Today, more than ever, we are aliens in our own land, worldview missionaries to our own post-Christian, postmodernist culture.
CHARLES COLSON

WE LIVE IN A SOCIETY today that is pluralistic in that it is made up of different ethnic, religious, and cultural groups. Our country embraces our individual differences and celebrates our individuality and our mutual desire for freedom. But the God of our lives is sovereign over everything.

God's sovereignty reigns over our professional lives, our personal lives, and our social calendar. All aspects of our lives are at their best when they reflect his character, and our role as Christians is to reflect that character throughout all aspects of our lives. Each aspect should be consistently and seamlessly related to God's Word. Our words and actions should reflect our faith.

The apostle Peter said, "Instead, you must worship Christ as Lord of your life. And if you are asked about your Christian hope, always be ready to explain it" (1 Pet. 3:15). As Christians we should be prepared to communicate the hope, grace, truth, and love of the gospel that is reflected in our own salvation and relationship with Christ.

A POST-CHRISTIAN WORLDVIEW

Unfortunately, this picture is not one we recognize when we look at present-day American culture. Our lives reflect more of the world than the Scriptures. The basic tenets of Christianity have been eliminated from the minds of many Americans. They are unfamiliar with even basic biblical teaching. Under such circumstances, the fabric of our country and its culture has no chance but to reflect the same changes.

In his book *How Now Shall We Live?*, Charles Colson explains that "no longer is the majority view the outlook of morally conservative, religious, patriotic middle America. . . . The worldview framed on campuses from the 1960's on has now entered the mainstream of American life." He added credence to this conclusion with a study completed in 1997 by *American Demographics* magazine. The results said there had been a "comprehensive shift in values, worldviews, and ways of life"[1] among approximately one-fourth of American adults. This set of Americans was found to embrace a new set of values that included "environmentalism, feminism, global issues, and spiritual searching."

Colson added his analysis of the study. He said that this new set of adults was found to "often have a background in movements for social justice, civil rights, feminism, and New Age spirituality. Thoroughly postmodernist, they are skeptical, if not resentful, of moral absolutes. They see 'nature as sacred' and emphasize self-actualization and spiritual growth."[2]

America is in a post-Christian period. Prevalent worldviews, as reflected in our culture around us, support this conclusion. "Post-Christian" does not suggest that Americans no longer profess to be Christians. Most Americans still do. But many Americans no longer claim a Judeo-Christian basis for their morality and motivation. Many Americans believe that truth is something they can debate and adapt according to social change. They have forgotten that truth is not something you decide on and personalize. Truth is something you encounter.

Certain words and phrases have overtaken the Ten Commandments as moral absolutes in our society. For example, _tolerance._ The word has been lifted to such a level of hysteria that no exception is tolerated. It has taken on such irrationality that one wonders if it is still acceptable to be intolerant of murderers and rapists?

Another word is _hate._ One thing is certain for yesterday, today, and forever. God loves all of us unconditionally. The Bible is clear that we are not to hate others. "Don't just pretend that you love others. Really love them. Hate what is wrong. Stand on the side of the good" (Rom. 12:9). But the word _hate_ has become a dangerous weapon. It is used to manipulate discussions of right and wrong. The Bible is clear. There is a role for hate. It is not in hating people. It is in hating "what is wrong."

Any discussion concerning the immorality of homosexual behavior is immediately met with cries of "hate speech." Mere recognition of right and wrong gets the same response: hate. To condemn what is morally wrong is now equivalent to "hate" in the eyes of many.

A dangerous and specific example is a reaction by the Clinton White House in condemning the Southern Baptist Convention in late 1999. The Baptists had made public their intent to share the gospel with Hindus, Jews, and Muslims. Incredibly, White House press secretary Joe Lockhart attacked the Baptists at a White House press briefing for what he described as "religious hatred." He said, "I think the President has made very clear from his view from any quarter, no matter what quarter, no matter what quarter it comes from, his views on religious tolerance, and how one of the greatest challenges going into the next century is dealing with intolerance, dealing with ethnic and religious hatred, and coming to grips with the long-held resentments between religions. So I think he's been very clear in his opposition to whatever organization, including the Southern Baptist, that perpetuate ancient religious hatred."[3]

The Clinton administration boiled down the Great Commission to the equivalent of a pattern of "ancient religious hatred." This is an accurate reflection of how far from a dominant Judeo-Christian set of values the country and its leaders have strayed as its worldview has shifted.

The late theologian Francis Schaeffer predicted the increasing intolerance for such language. He called it hidden censorship. In his book, *The Christian Manifesto,* Schaeffer recognized the failure of Christians to slow the moral decline of the country. He asked, "Where have the Bible-believing Christians been in the last 40 years? . . . There has been a vast silence."

In a speech to the Coral Ridge Presbyterian Church in 1982, Schaeffer extended his challenge to the Christian community. "I wonder what God has to say to us? All these freedoms we have. All the secondary blessings we've had out of the preaching of the Gospel and we have let it slip through our fingers in the lifetime of most of you here." He added, "It's not only the Christian leaders. Where have the Christian lawyers been? . . . Where have the Christian doctors been— speaking out against the rise of abortion clinics and all the other things? Where have the Christian businessmen been—to put their lives and their work on the line concerning these things which they would say as Christians are central to them? Where have the Christian educators been—as we have lost our educational system? Where have they been? Where have each of you been?"[4]

Christians are dual citizens. We are first citizens of the kingdom of God, bought and paid for with the blood of Jesus Christ. We are also citizens of the world we live in and are commissioned to live the life of Christ in our actions and deeds while in this world. This duality of citizenship leads to situations that can be characterized as contradictory.

How can Christians show love and live among all of the sin in the world without showing hate and intolerance?

In her book _Light in the City_, national radio host Janet Parshall also referred to Schaeffer. The Christian church "needed to perfect the practice of the truth of God. This, he [Schaeffer] observed, required the loving confrontation of antithesis—we must proclaim and stand for God's truth—and in so doing confront 'what is false in theology, in the church, and the surrounding culture.' . . . None of us relish confrontation. Yet if we live out the practice of truth in a culture built, more and more, on distortion, manipulation, and hedonism, we must enter into confrontation. We must practice love in that confrontation. But we must also practice truth."[5]

A CALL FOR RENEWAL OF PURPOSE

When it comes to the management of financial assets inside the Christian community, there must be a confrontation of truth. Christians have unwittingly been capitalizing anti-family businesses for decades with billions of dollars while spending millions of dollars fighting many of the same issues in the political arena. Truth must be confronted by Christian individuals, financial professionals, and those with the responsibility of managing money in foundations, endowments, funds, and retirement plans funded by Christians.

No longer can ignorance of the ability to screen out offensive companies be an acceptable excuse to not implement it. Those who fund such ministries must confront the truth. For example, contributors to that national pro-life ministry should rise up against it unless the ministry leaders promise to divest from pro-abortion businesses and companies. Money managers representing significant pools of money should be ashamed if they do not have adequate and professional measures in place to screen their funds on behalf of contributors who expect as much.

Christian organizations must begin to take the time to sort through marketing phrases like "ethical" and "spiritual" when describing investment methods to really understand what they mean. Slick marketing language must be viewed through a theological filter to understand the true screening standards. Are investment screening philosophies that are based on good works and backed up by the Dalai Lama really the kind of worldview you want your portfolio to reflect?

Amazingly, billions of Christian-based dollars are already invested through screening programs that represent thinly veiled agendas promoting a naturalist worldview. Certainly, in many cases no screening at all might be preferable to investments in businesses that advance an antithetical worldview to Christianity.

Christian-based ministries and organizations must recognize that choosing not to screen their investment assets in an obedient integration of their faith is still a choice. Just as a political decision to stay home from the polls and not vote could actually end up helping a candidate win, a choice to avoid screening could result in some portfolio assets—whether your personal ones or ones you are hired to manage—being invested in and supporting anti-family companies.

Consider these examples: companies like Eidos, that poison our children through video games depicting murder, decapitation, and obscene language mixed with intense eroticism and scenes of sexual bondage; companies like Abercrombie & Fitch, that put photos of nude women and tips for getting sex in college in general clothing catalogs; companies like Hewlett-Packard, that funded a foundation to provide a $10-million loan to a Chinese manufacturing plant to produce the heinous RU-486 spontaneous abortion pill; companies like Merrill Lynch, that chooses to pull funding from the Boy Scouts of America because a court approved its right to restrict gay men from being Scout leaders.

Christians must recognize that it is impossible to stay on the sidelines and not get involved. Companies today create and promote clear agendas whether we want to accept them or not. Some companies do it in pursuit of money and market share. Other companies pursue agendas as an extension of the worldview of their management and boards of directors. Either way, when you invest with some companies, you are partnering with an agenda to influence our culture that is as real as sending money to a political candidate who tries to legislate the same agenda.

As a hypothetical example, suppose a national Christian ministry were to send a $100,000 political contribution to Congressman Barney Frank. Other Christians and the ministry's contributors would be outraged because Frank is a vociferous advocate of the right to abortion on demand and for sweeping special rights for gays and lesbians.

Should there be less outrage if the same ministry invests $1 million in Viacom, which uses shareholder money to contribute to Planned Parenthood? Viacom also sponsored the 2000 GLAAD (Gay and Lesbian Alliance against Defamation) Media Awards and is ranked thirtieth in the country for gay-friendly and pro-gay and lesbian companies by Gay Financial Network. As far as I know, Frank hasn't been peddling any pornography to the public lately while Viacom certainly has. It has made and distributed movies like *Virtual Girl,* its erotic MTV programming, and the toilet-humor show and movie *South Park.* In truth, there should be more outrage at Viacom than at Barney Frank.

I challenge Christians to reject the dual life of living within the world six and a half days of the week when they are not in church. Reject the notion that the daily decisions you make at work and at home do not reflect your heart's love for Christ. An influential Quaker teacher named Elton Trueblood once said, "It is hard to exaggerate the degree to which the modern church seems irrelevant to modern man."

Reject this irrelevance. Embrace a new commitment to be salt and light. We must emphasize building up Christian professionals as much as professional Christians. Why have Christian values not been relevant to Christian money managers over the past decades the same way that naturalist values have been so important to environmentalists and humanists? We must integrate our worldview into everyday life just as effectively as they. As Francis Schaeffer said, "Where have the Christian financial professionals been?" When it comes to integrating our worldview into our work lives, into our daily decisions involving relationships, politics, and money, we are falling short.

Christians have experimented with taking their worldview into the political arena with mixed success. We should each individually take our worldview into our professions, our relationships, and into the influence of our financial assets. Whose assets are they anyway? The truth is that we own none of it. Everything we have is a blessing from God.

Imagine for a moment that God told you you were being given $100,000 to manage directly for him. How much more seriously would you accept the responsibility than you do your own assets? Would you take it more seriously than managing assets for a church, a church college, or a church ministry? Would you feel comfortable investing any of God's money into Disney, AT&T, Viacom, Seagrams, Playboy, or other mainstream companies? Would you feel comfortable attempting to explain to God that you felt by owning Disney, Seagrams, and Playboy you would be able to earn more money so you could tithe more of it to the church?

Of course not. God can make all the money he wants. But what he wants from us is obedience to his Word. What he wants from us is to understand from Scripture that our actions have consequences far beyond the value of a higher rate of return. He wants us to integrate a worldview that embraces his teachings into our daily lives—and that includes the management of our money.

DIFFERENT WORLDVIEWS
REQUIRE DIFFERENT MEASUREMENTS

As Christians living within the world, we are challenged to deny the world's measurement of success. Our culture tells us that larger houses, vacation homes, foreign cars, tailored clothes, nannies, foreign vacations, impressive titles, and plastic surgery are all measures of success.

The Bible is very clear that God is not impressed with materialism. Our eternal rewards will not be based on the empires of materialism that we can amass on Earth. The Bible warns us about the futility of chasing the world's measurements of success:

- "Those who love money will never have enough. How absurd to think that wealth brings true happiness! The more you have, the more people come to help you spend it. So what is the advantage of wealth—except perhaps to watch it run through your fingers!" (Eccles. 5:10–11).

- "Then he said, 'Beware! Don't be greedy for what you don't have. Real life is not measured by how much we own'" (Luke 12:15).

- "Tell those who are rich in this world not to be proud and not to trust in their money, which will soon be gone. But their trust should be in the living God, who richly gives us all we need for our enjoyment. Tell them to use their money to do good. They should be rich in good works and should give generously to those in need, always being ready to share with others whatever God has given them. By doing this they will be storing up their treasure as a good foundation for the future so that they may take hold of real life" (1 Tim. 6:17–19).

In the same fashion, Christians who are responsible for managing the investment of their own money or the money of other Christians in a church, ministry, or foundation also cannot use the world's measurement of success. The world says that the highest rates of return without regard for anything else defines success as an investment manager, and other variables are secondary, like cost, volatility, and duration of track record.

For Christians living in the world, our measurement of successful investing must be different from the world's. Larry Burkett, the noted Christian financial author and president of Christian Financial Concepts, refers to Colossians 3:17 in defining successful investing in a Christian worldview: "And whatever you do or say, let it be as a representative of the Lord Jesus, all the while giving thanks through him to God the Father."

"Because everything we do witnesses to what we believe, some investments will be unacceptable to us (Christians). All Christians should thoroughly check into how their money is being used," Burkett says. With his own experience investing in mutual funds, he "found some funds were investing in such activities as abortion and pornographic literature." He says he supports the investigation of whether any company invested in "is using any visible proportion of its resources to support anti-Christian causes."[6]

For a ministry to receive a high rate of investment return through enriching companies like Playboy, the World Wrestling Federation, and Rick's Cabaret redefines the effort from successful in the world's eye to quite unsuccessful in the context of a Christian worldview. The end does not justify the means because God is in control of the end. It is the "means" that tests our faith and our obedience in our Christian walk. The "means" of how high investment rates of return are attained must be recognized for our own worldviews.

It is time for Christians to come out of the closet and defend the definition of investment success in terms of our own worldview. As the naturalists have become accepted for determining their own measures of success according to their own naturalist worldview through socially responsible investing, Christians must strive for the same.

The Christian worldview predates any other, and the Christian community is as large as any other in this country and has as much or more collective assets tied to it as any other special interest group. As I have met and worked with hundreds of Christian financial professionals across the country over the past years, I have seen a distinct identity crisis when it comes to challenging Wall Street to accept our unique worldview. This individual meekness frustrates me. Some cream-of-the-crop financial advisers in this country are unwilling to come out of the closet with their professional peers and with their customers.

I have said to many of them, "Letting someone know that you are a Christian does not need to disqualify you from your professional ability to manage money." We serve the Prince of peace and the King of kings, and yet many of us are intimidated to let anyone know about it, much less use the positions and skills God has given us to represent him and a worldview based on his Word.

Have you heard the story of the godly man who was disappointed because he thought God broke a promise to him? He said, "Lord, you promised me that I would win the lottery this week so I could use the winnings to fund all of our church missionary programs. They picked the numbers, and I didn't win. Lord, how could this happen?"

God responded to the man: "Look, I did my part. It would have helped if you simply would have purchased a lottery ticket."

The story reminds me of how we have overlooked the potential influence of the blessings God has already given us. We have the financial resources to make a difference in this world as witnesses for Christ. Yet we are not yet effectively using those blessings to confront the world in which we live.

The late Bob Briner said it's time to be bold:

> We don't need to take the rap that we're just a
> bunch of do-gooders who need to be placated now and
> then by highly publicized visits with the president or an

occasional feature story in the local newspaper on one
of our many conventions or crusades. We don't need to
take the palliatives from our leaders who tell us, Don't
expect too much when we decide to get involved in
positive, constructive ways in our communities. . . . We
don't have to sit back and wring our hands at the way
our culture is going down the drain. We don't have to
be content with a position on the sidelines when our
Lord has assigned us a starting role on the winning
team. . . . We need to reclaim the territory, not in a tri-
umphalistic sense, but out of a strong conviction that
this is where we belong.[7]

Our call to action is not to take it upon ourselves to change the
world. Our call to action can be summed up as follows:
- Humbly accept our shortcomings with the blessings God has
given us in using them for his glory.
- Obediently accept the challenge to integrate an active Christian
worldview with our financial decisions while we are still citizens
of this world.
- Lift our country and our culture, and our efforts to positively
impact it, in prayer to God.
- Pray for changing hearts in America, for ultimately, only
changed hearts will transform our culture back to a Christian
worldview.
- Commit our efforts to God, for our efforts will be in vain without the strength and power of God working through us.

With God's hand and our obedience, roaring lambs will positively
influence Wall Street to uplift our culture and our families in the
present-day post-Christian world.

CHAPTER 13

THE CHRISTIAN INVESTOR GUIDEBOOK

> The only thing
> necessary for
> the triumph of
> evil is for
> good men to
> do nothing.
> EDMUND BURKE

CULTURE WARRIOR William Bennett identified the starting point for confronting today's post-Christian culture—you and me. "The hard truth is that in a free society the ultimate responsibility rests with the people themselves. It is our beliefs, our behavior, and our philosophy that have in many instances changed for the worse. Our injury is self-inflicted; the good news is that what has been self-inflicted can be self-corrected."[1]

We can make a difference. We have a responsibility to take such actions simply out of obedience. This begins with you and me making everyday financial decisions that take the values of our investments into consideration. Whether it is a simple investment in an individual retirement account, or whether you are a professional investment manager who directs millions of dollars, your daily decisions will make a difference.

Using your investment assets to influence the culture is great in theory but will work effectively only if there is a credible and sophisticated database of research on America's companies. Before investors can choose to clean their portfolios of cultural pollution, those companies

173

that are cultural polluters must be identified. Once identified and confirmed, there is also a terrific challenge in making this information accessible to investors across the country. This information allows investors to avoid investing in offensive companies and to choose alternative clean companies that offer just as good or better investment rates of return. The values-based investing movement, while still very young, has already gone through tremendous growing pains in order to mature to the stage where an abundance of data and information is available to both individual and professional investors alike.

VBI—In the Beginning

Much like the socially responsible investing movement, the values-based investing movement started with a number of individual pioneers who followed a passion. The passion was to create a model that would allow people to invest in a way that was consistent with their personal convictions. In this case, the common set of convictions centered on Christian principles. Each of the early pioneers found a different business plan to support the goal of creating a Christian-based screening protocol and database. There were large discrepancies between what issues were being screened, what was important and what wasn't, and how the services were marketed.

The earliest flirtations with values-based investing occurred as a tangent from the early socially responsible investing movement. There were some mutual funds that chose to screen out alcohol and tobacco products. Fund families like the Pioneer group and the Templeton group quietly avoided alcohol and tobacco but never marketed their funds by highlighting their screens.

Two early mutual fund players on the scene reflected the wide variance in defining what issues were important to Christians when it came to values-based investing. The MMA Praxis Fund (sponsored by the Mennonite Mutual Aid Association) first arrived on the market on

January 4, 1994. It was marketed as a fund that represented Christian values, but it took a wide latitude with what that meant. The fund had no policy on domestic partner benefits or companies using money to support gay or nonmarried heterosexual lifestyles. Nor did it have any comprehensive abortion policies and, in fact, recognized Planned Parenthood as an important social benefit organization. The funds placed much more focus on the standard alcohol, tobacco, and gambling screens. (See chap. 8 for more information.)

Less than three months later, in March 1994, came a fund called the Timothy Plan. Based in Orlando, Florida, the Timothy Plan was created by a former Shearson branch manager named Art Ally. It was the first mutual fund to represent a strict adherence to Christian values in its representation as a values-based investing alternative to socially responsible investing. The Timothy Plan did not have the luxury of having a built-in distribution system like the MMA Praxis Funds did. It grew very slowly. Compared to the overall mutual fund industry, the fund had very few marketing dollars to get its message out.

The fund also had the misfortune of choosing a few money managers early on who disabled its reputation with very poor investment performance. However, the bad performance was not related to the screening restrictions. In other words, there was a perceived fear that the Timothy Plan discipline cut out so many companies that the only ones left were those that didn't make any money. Unfortunately, this is exactly what many investors concluded. Because Timothy was the first to take a strict view of screening, it was assumed that the high number of restricted companies inherently led to poor investment performance.

Rudimentary analysis suggested otherwise. Regardless of the screening restrictions, it is extraordinarily difficult for a new mutual fund, started with a small amount of money, to attract a first-class money manager and thus grow large enough to reduce its costs and expense

ratios. In addition to money manager problems, the fund had catego-
rized itself in a certain class of stocks that remained out of favor in the
market for a number of years. The Timothy Plan is classified as a
"small-cap value fund." This means that the portfolio manager will
seek only companies that are smaller in size (as measured by market
capitalization, hence small-cap) and those that are selected by a "value"
methodology of analysis as opposed to a "growth" methodology. For its
early years, small-cap value stocks as a whole significantly underperformed other segments of the market. On top of that, Timothy's
money manager underperformed even the small-cap value averages.

This poor performance and the relatively small size of the Timothy
Plan created a bad first impression among ministries and Christian
organizations on the ability of values-based investing to be competitive
with investment returns while cleaning up the values of the companies
in the portfolio.

Independent research on companies was impossible to get. I saw a
great need for creating an independent database of research on America's
companies from a values-based investing perspective. With much prayer
and family support, I began building the first such research group in
1994. The task seemed so enormous that it appeared impossible. It had
been a passion burning in my heart for more than ten years. I would
continually talk about it with my wife, Joni. She told me she heard news
reports that supported our contentions that some corners of corporate
America were degrading our culture without any resistance.

Two events ultimately led me to create the first independent
research organization committed to promoting the embryonic values-
based investing movement. The first was a simple dinner with my wife.
In another intense discussion about what "could be and should be"
done about Christians being wiser about investing their money, Joni
blurted out, in the way only a loving wife can, "Scott, I'm tired of talking about what should be done. If we're going to keep talking about

this, let's do something about it. And if we're going to do something about it, let's do something about it right now."

I knew she was right.

The second event occurred a few months later and was much more bizarre. Joni and I were in New York City to visit with some mutual fund managers. During a free afternoon in our schedule, Joni and I were seeking shelter from a heavy rainstorm. We were shopping in the mall at Rockefeller Center. While moving from one store to another, I was approached by an NBC representative. He asked me if I would like to see the Donohue show. Although we didn't understand why someone just picked me out of the crowd, after some discussion we agreed to see the show.

What happened over the next hour shocked me to such an extent that I was convicted even more than before to follow my passion. Once I was escorted to the studio, I was asked to actually sit at a table on the stage while my wife was offered a front-row seat behind me. It turned out that the show was about the revival of "go-go girls" in Manhattan. In effect, I was used as an audience for eight consecutive strippers as they came out and did their stripping routine in front of me throughout the show.

It was outrageous. While I had heard that daytime television had become a cesspool, I had not known how bad it was. Believe me. Even after being heavily edited for broadcast, the show I was a part of was really soft pornography. I immediately understood the phrase that Senator Joe Lieberman had coined about parents rising up against daytime TV programming. He called it "the revolt of the revolted."

Well, Joni and I were both revolted. And it was time to do some revolting.

Soon after, the Institute for American Values was launched to empower investors with information on the cultural values of America's corporations. The institute received early national press attention. CNBC called me "the new kid on the block" of issues-based investing. Newspapers from the *New York Times* to the *San Diego Union Tribune* covered the new "conservative alternative" for investors across the country.

The national attention helped solidify the notion that culturally conservative people of faith had an interest in entirely different issues than those represented by standard socially responsible investing disciplines. Finally, there was an acceptance that the SRI movement did not accurately serve the core screening needs of the Christian and culturally conservative communities.

Two more mutual funds joined the movement. In May 1996, Bill Van Allen started the Noah Fund, a mutual fund that screened for many of the new values-based investing issues. Van Allen was able to retain a top-tier money manager to manage the tiny fund from the beginning. The Noah Fund began and has remained as the top performing VBI fund, based on investment rate of return.

Also, the Catholic Values Investment Trust focused mainly on abortion screens while also including screening for pornography and anti-family entertainment. This fund attracted sizable investments through Catholic institutions and offered screening for those who wanted their investments to be consistent with their pro-life views.

One of the challenges within the young and narrow values-based investing industry has been coming to terms with creating and managing standard definitions. Each of the funds developed its own screening data with different qualities of acquisition, procedures, and processes. What represented an abortion screen with one did not conform to the definition of an abortion screen with another.

VBI—THE FOUNDATION IS SET

For investors to effectively use their assets as tools in the culture war, there needed to be more resources for them. Financial products and a research database had to be developed. These are the tools that give investors choices. By learning from many of the mistakes of the early socially responsible investing movement, the resources have become readily available for investors today for making values-based investing choices.

As the individual factions within this movement have begun working together, more standardization of cultural screen definitions has developed. This allows investors to know exactly what a screen means and what kinds of companies it will impact. Precise screen parameters lead to a more precise consequence to the companies that ultimately stand to lose investment dollars and support.

While most values-based investing databases still offer the traditional three screens of alcohol, tobacco, and gambling, the unique screens also cover various aspects of the abortion business, pornography, anti-family entertainment, and nonmarried lifestyles.

These new screens relate directly to the issues that most people of faith today see as degrading our culture and threatening the integrity of our country and our families. By accurately identifying which companies are choosing to profit with these issues at the expense of our culture, Christians can better use their investments to engage the culture. (For a detailed review of the individual screening definitions, please refer to the appendix.)

VBI—Looking over the Horizon

Values-based investing is now poised to offer individual Christian investors and church, parachurch, and ministry-related institutional money managers the opportunity to access accurate and sophisticated data in order to avoid companies that pollute our culture. The depth of the data and the number of VBI-related financial products and services available today also means that there is no need to believe you must sacrifice your investment rate of return to do so. More financial products are becoming available. Access to data and research is available for free. Top Wall Street money managers in some cases are also offering values-based investing services.

Most of the individual leaders in the values-based investing movement, from mutual fund managers and stock brokers to research analysts, are now meeting together in a common discourse to work together through a common message. Even though organizations may differ on the specifics of their personal values-based methodologies, the movement has matured to the level that the organizations are working in tandem. The common message is obedience to God in using our assets to reflect the Christian worldview.

At the same time, some large ministries are beginning to embrace the movement. Concerned Women for America has changed its investments through screens. Recently, the Christian Stewardship Association has agreed to create a series of screened mutual funds with a top-tier investment management firm based in Houston, Texas. The Assemblies of God denomination was a pioneer in implementing the VBI discipline through its foundation investments. The Presbyterian Church of America is considering the integration of screening in its investment philosophies.

But the vast majority of Christian organizations and investors have yet to make a commitment to using their investment assets to engage the culture. For every positive example, there are dozens of examples of ministries and advocacy groups like the National Right to Life organization that disavow any need for screening. Even after being directly challenged in writing by a contributor, the National Right to Life president made no response or acknowledgement of the fact that this ministry owned securities that were involved in the business of, or direct support of, abortion.

Another common pitfall of ministries is a false self-confidence that their own internal resources are adequate to take care of any potential problems. Certainly, it can be risky for a ministry to be vulnerable enough to admit that it has not invested time in creating, finding, or retaining the sophisticated research needed to effectively implement a screening program. But like anything else, a weakness cannot be properly addressed until it is recognized.

I encountered this situation with a well-known international ministry. In the course of completing research for this book, it had been alleged to me that this ministry had been offered a program to initiate a values-based investing program for its own robust investment portfolio but had flatly turned away from the philosophy it represented.

In fairness, I offered the leader the opportunity to respond to the allegation. After further research I learned, contrary to the allegation, that the ministry took steps internally to emphasize values-based investing principles on all of its investing decisions. A ministry official told me that the leader and founder had himself reiterated a ministry-wide mandate to honor its contributors and avoid un-Christian investment choices.

While I was very pleased to see this ministry join the ranks of those taking a leadership role in this movement, another statement to me reflected a simplistic approach. I was told that the ministry's board was sufficient to provide moral investment advice without needing an outside consultant.

Such a statement is endemic among Christian organizations that believe a deep knowledge of Scripture, theology, and political culture also leads to a deep knowledge of how multinational corporations are making and using their corporate cash. Such a statement reflects a fundamental lack of understanding of what is at stake. Of course, I am not questioning the impeccable credentials of the ministry's board. I am, however, questioning its ability to have in-depth knowledge of how thousands of American companies score in a values-based investing measurement.

This would be akin to believing that just because a board of directors was theologically astute it would automatically know the intricacies of any proposed legislation on Capitol Hill that may impact families and our culture. Of course, it would be impossible to keep up on such information without great attention or professional assistance. The same is true with values-based investing and the nature of what companies stand for and represent.

Even though, as one ministry told me, it "would never knowingly support firms that advocate abortion, pornography, gambling, or anti-family lifestyles," it is not enough to simply say that you will only screen out that which you are aware of. The point is that millions of Christians unknowingly support cultural polluters. Ministries must take this as seriously as they do public policy matters and make a serious effort to strip away any ownership of companies that do not honor God's Word. My hope is that all ministries will recognize this and quickly move beyond their existing internal knowledge and choose to use their investment capital to engage the culture around us.

In fact, despite great efforts, the vast majority of financial professionals who have responsibility for investing some of the nation's largest Christian ministries still have no grasp or understanding of the methodology. I was recently invited to speak to a number of chief financial officers and treasurers for some of the largest ministries in Colorado Springs, Colorado. Together, the nearly two dozen financial officers represented hundreds of millions of dollars of investment capital. Although there was a lot of enthusiasm for the idea once it was presented, it was clear that these Christian leaders had previously not grasped the responsibility in front of them regarding values-based screening.

There is much work to be done. Investors and ministries need rudimentary guidelines to adopt values-based investing with their financial decisions. Whether novices or professionals, they can become roaring lambs among the bulls and bears of Wall Street.

PRACTICAL STEPS TO BEGIN
A VALUES-BASED INVESTING PROGRAM

To begin integrating this new philosophy into your personal and professional investing discipline, I have created a guide consisting of steps, resources, and tools to help you. Before you can be an effective values-based investor, you must be a good investor. The following sage advice from investment professionals and Christian financial experts can help you become a prudent and successful investor.

STAGE ONE: THE FIRST-TIME INVESTOR

If you are just starting an investment program, you will need to make sure that you have a grasp of basic investment knowledge. You should also make sure you are grounded in scriptural lessons on investing. The Scriptures have a lot to say about money. There are more than twenty-three hundred references to money and possessions in the Bible. So the best place to start is to make sure your financial strategies are biblically based.

In Luke, God tells us that unless the area of money is under God's authority, no other area will be. "'Unless you are faithful in small matters, you won't be faithful in large ones. If you cheat even a little, you won't be honest with greater responsibilities. And if you are untrustworthy about worldly wealth, who will trust you with the true riches of heaven? And if you are not faithful with other people's money, why should you be trusted with money of your own? No one can serve two masters. For you will hate one and love the other, or be devoted to one and despise the other. You cannot serve both God and money'" (Luke 16:10–13).

My purpose is not to cover general financial planning strategies and concepts. I would like to recommend what I consider to be the all-star list of Christian-based financial resources on general planning, saving, and investing. General principles you can use are:

- "Depend on and trust in God.
- Handle money responsibly.
- Give generously.
- Save mightily.
- Work industriously.
- Invest wisely."[2]

If you are a new or first-time investor, here is a list of top resources to use in building your financial foundation from a biblical perspective. I recommend these books:

- *Sound Mind Investing: A Step-by-Step Guide to Financial Stability and Growth* by Austin Pryor
- *The Christian's Guide to Worry-Free Money Management* by Daniel Busby, Kent Barber, and Robert Temple
- *Investing for the Future* by Larry Burkett
- *Your Finances in Changing Times* by Larry Burkett
- *Master Your Money* by Ron Blue

You could also try the software "Money Matters 2000" by Crown Financial Ministries.

Christian-based financial Web sites to choose from are:

- The Money Channel at Crosswalk.com—www.crosswalk.com
- Sound Mind Investing—www.sminow.com
- Crown Financial Ministries—www.crown.org

STAGE TWO: THE EXPERIENCED PERSONAL INVESTOR

As an experienced investor, you should take these steps right away to begin your path to a pollution-free investment portfolio.

Step A: Take inventory of what cultural issues are important to you. As I have detailed throughout this book, there are a number of issues to be concerned about when you tailor a portfolio to your own personal criteria. Take some quiet time to consider which of the four cultural screens (abortion, pornography, anti-family entertainment, and non-married lifestyles) and the three consumer screens (alcohol, tobacco, and gambling) are important to you and your family. Which combination of these screens represents a Christian worldview for you?

Step B: Determine your own personal tolerance level. Some investors are "purist" investors. In other words, even if the portfolio is worth $500,000, not one penny should be invested in any offensive company, whether individually or via a packaged financial product like a mutual fund.

Other investors believe that on a pragmatic basis some exposure is justifiable. In this example, an investor who has $25,000 of an overall $500,000 portfolio invested in a mutual fund may not be led to selling the mutual fund if the fund held only $500 worth of Disney stock. In this case, while Disney would make up only 2.0 percent of the mutual fund, it would make up only 0.1 percent of the portfolio as a whole. Determine an overall tolerance level for investments in offending companies. Whether it is 5 percent or 15 percent, you will then have a benchmark to use as a guide in making decisions that include the values of the companies you own.

Step C: Choose a source for your values information. Decisions made on bad information are still bad decisions. Choose which source of data and information you will use to gauge the values of any company holding. If you cannot find one that suits you, create your own personal investigation system through resources on the Internet or in the public library. Make certain that the worldview of the organization creating the data is consistent with your own.

Do not accept labels such as "ethical" or "spiritual" or "socially responsible" to automatically be consistent with your own worldview. Much of the mainstream socially responsible investing research and information has its roots in a naturalism worldview. While it may

PUT YOUR MONEY WHERE YOUR MORALS ARE

espouse a concern to screen out alcohol, tobacco, and gambling, the true philosophy and impact of the screens employed are to promote humankind's own ultimate solution for all problems in the determined absence of God.

As another example, there are socially liberal groups that still call their screens "pro-life," but ultimately they screen out only companies that manufacture birth control products or condoms. You must look deeper than the label to ensure that the data you are basing your decisions on represent your worldview. A listing of potential sources for this data is in the appendix of this book.

Step D: Take a "values audit" of your existing portfolio. Review the existing stocks, mutual funds, and annuities you have under the focus of the values screens you have selected. Measure your score in terms of dollars invested. For example, assume you are measuring the following sample portfolio:

Shares	Company	Symbol	Price per share	Total dollars invested
300	Micron Technology	MU	40	$12,000
300	American Home Products	AHP	61	$18,300
300	Toys "R" Us	TOY	15	$4,500
300	Cabot Oil & Gas	COG	20	$6,000
300	American Skiing Co.	SKI	2	$600
			Total Dollars Invested	$41,400

One of the five holdings is involved in practices that would be offensive to cultural conservatives. That holding is American Home Products. The company manufactures pharmaceutical products that are used as abortifacients and makes contributions to Planned Parenthood.

The analysis of this portfolio should not be that 20 percent of your portfolio is involved in offensive activities (one out of five companies).

Rather, you need to analyze your portfolio by actual dollars invested. You have $18,300 invested in an offensive company out of the $41,400 total. Even though only 20 percent of your holdings (one in five stocks) is offensive, 44.2 percent of your actual dollars invested is in a business offensive to you.

Compare your final score to the tolerance level you have chosen. If you have decided that you can live with a portfolio that cumulatively has no more than 15 percent of its assets in offensive companies, then the example portfolio clearly fails your personal test.

Step E: Make changes to your portfolio. Using the same example, your next step would be to change your portfolio to make it in line with your convictions and tolerance levels. If you must divest of an existing holding, then you need to search for an alternative stock that is clean, that is in the same industry, and that also has the same or better investment performance potential. In this example, you would divest of American Home Products. Many clean pharmaceutical companies would represent appropriate substitutions. An example is Abbott Laboratories. Abbott could be purchased to take the place of American Home Products, and your portfolio would be reconstructed with no negative financial implications.

The investment integrity of the portfolio remains intact since you have replaced a pharmaceutical company with another pharmaceutical company, keeping the diverse exposure to various industries in your portfolio unaltered. Because Abbott has comparable forecasts for earnings, there is no reason to believe that your overall investment performance will be negatively affected. And finally, the cultural integrity of your portfolio has been restored.

Step F: Communicate your decision. If you are in a position to sell any holdings, you have the opportunity to expand the impact of your decision beyond that of your portfolio. As I discussed in an earlier chapter, companies are very sensitive to policies or products that may lead to investors selling their stock and driving the stock price down.

If you sell a stock, you should write a very respectful letter to the director of investor relations of that company. Tell the person why you have chosen to divest from his or her company and that you would consider reinvesting should the company ever choose to change its policies or dump offensive products. Give your name and address. You will be surprised at how many personal responses you will get. Collectively, however, you will be increasing the awareness of major companies that there is a cost to them if they choose to become involved in anti-family business practices. (A sample letter and recommendations on where to get mailing information are in the appendix.)

If you sell from a mutual fund instead of a stock, you should write the same kind of letter directly to the mutual fund manager. You will be an important influence on the manager next time he considers buying that same company in his portfolio. He may likely remember that by holding that stock in his mutual fund portfolio, he takes the risk of driving more customers away to clean competitors. (Similarly, a sample letter is in the appendix.)

STAGE THREE: THE INSTITUTIONAL INVESTOR FOR CHRISTIAN ORGANIZATIONS

The person who manages the assets of a church, parachurch ministry, church college, retirement plan, or any large pool of money in which the assets were gathered from contributions in the name of Christ has special responsibility.

In addition to the traditional fiduciary responsibilities, this person must be accountable for appropriate stewardship entrusted to him or her on behalf of Christians who have given their money as contributions. This stewardship responsibility must include the consideration of active values-based screening for all the portfolio's contents.

Step A: A cultural policy is needed in the investment policy statement. An investment policy statement (IPS) details the foundation on which all future investment decisions within the portfolio are made. The document establishes portfolio goals, clarifies investment guidelines, and identifies investment parameters and monitoring benchmarks. An IPS is essentially a business plan or blueprint for investing portfolio assets as well as an insurance guideline for money managers to make sure they follow predetermined guidelines to avoid investment pitfalls.

Typically thought of in conjunction with the portfolios of qualified retirement plans, charitable institutions, or trusts—situations in which a fiduciary directs investment activities—an IPS is one of the first steps taken in managing the investments of any portfolio. For fiduciary-directed portfolios, the IPS provides a benchmark to determine whether the fiduciary is making prudent investment decisions and ensures a continuity of investment strategies for a portfolio managed by an investment committee.

In this context, you should add a cultural policy section to your IPS. This will be the same as determining your "tolerance level" as described previously. However, the cultural policy section will do more. For example, the organization your portfolio represents may have tailored interests when it comes to specific cultural screens. The cultural policy section should identify which screens will be used and which overall tolerance level (if greater than zero) will be acceptable to the portfolio. If the organization agrees that having less than 5 percent of the portfolio invested in companies that fail the screens is OK, then the cultural policy needs to dictate that fact.

This section will then inform the money manager, or set of money managers, about the measurable guidelines and parameters. This is a critical step to present to your contributors as evidence of active stewardship over the money you manage. (A sample investment policy statement with a cultural policy section can be found in the appendix.)

Step B: Audit, divest, and communicate. The following steps for institutional investing are the very same as those identified in the previous section for experienced personal investors. Once a cultural policy section has been added to your IPS, you should then audit your existing portfolio using the screens and guidelines you have chosen. Once you have the audit report, you should make any divestments that are needed and replace any stocks that were sold with clean stocks within the same asset class and with comparable investment performance potential. Finally, you should exercise your influence as an institutional money manager to communicate with those companies whose stock you sold and tell them you are no longer comfortable owning their stock because of their anti-family products and policies.

A FINAL THOUGHT

For years the Lord put a burden on my heart to pursue the development of the values-based investing research and movement. I was living in a small city in the Northwest at the time. There was no logical reason for me to leave my profession, uproot my family, and spend my personal money to walk through the doors that seemed open in front of me. I had two choices: providing for my family and maintaining order in my life or walking away from my career to pursue my passion.

In an effort to seek God's will for my family and me, I sought counsel from a few friends at church and other people I respected. One person I sought out was Jeff Kemp, the brilliant director of the Washington Family Council based in Seattle, Washington. Kemp has both the wit and the voice of his famous father, Jack.

After hearing me talk (and probably whine a little), he assessed the situation quickly with stunning effectiveness. I told him that people in my home church told me I was crazy to take such risks. I also told him that I questioned why I should pursue such a risky plan when my family and I were so comfortable.

Kemp looked straight at me and said, "Scott, let me ask you: When was the last time that the Lord's will was in your comfort zone?"

His question seared through me with the conviction of the Holy Spirit. Of course this was not about comfort zones. This wasn't about keeping order in my family's life. This was about obedience. This was about accepting God's invitation to be used as a vessel. What an extraordinary privilege it was. I will always thank Jeff Kemp for the godly wisdom he passed on to me that rainy morning.

Today I take the opportunity to pass on Jeff Kemp's challenge to you. As you consider adding values-based screening to your financial decisions, perhaps you don't want to take the extra time and analysis it would require. Perhaps you are uncomfortable with the perceived risk of accepting a lower rate of return by selling offensive holdings. Is it possible that you are uncomfortable with the thought of finding out just how bad your existing investments might be culturally? Maybe you are just comfortable with a system that, in your mind, "isn't broken."

Let me ask you: When was the last time the Lord's will was in your comfort zone?

RESOURCES AND DATA FOR THE VALUES-BASED INVESTOR

LISTS

Then David continued, "Be strong and courageous, and do the work. Don't be afraid or discouraged by the size of the task, for the LORD God, my God, is with you. He will not fail you or forsake you. He will see to it that all the work related to the Temple of the LORD is finished correctly."
1 CHRONICLES 28:20

The following lists analyzing mutual funds are based on this criterion: investment quality ratings are provided by Morningstar from the latest publicly available information as of October 2000 (one star is the lowest value; five, the highest). This information can be updated for free by going to www.morningstar.com. The clean ratings are based on the latest portfolio and values-based investing research as of October 2000. Each score is based on the decision to screen out all companies that fail the following seven screens: (1) alcohol, (2) tobacco, (3) gambling, (4) abortion, (5) anti-family entertainment, (6) pornography, and (7) nonmarried lifestyles. Results can change if you take any one or more of the seven screening criteria. This information can be updated for free by going to http://money.crosswalk.com/investigator.

ANALYSIS OF "RELIGIOUS-SCREENED" MUTUAL FUNDS

Fund Name/Affiliation	Morningstar Quality Rating	% of Portfolio Is Clean	Overall Grade
Aquinas Balanced Fund (Catholic)	3 Stars	85%	C-
Aquinas Equity Growth	4 Stars	65%	D
Aquinas Equity Income	2 Stars	64%	F
Capstone SERV Large Cap (Adventist)	Not Rated	40%	F
Capstone SERV Small Cap	Not Rated	98%	A
Catholic Values Equity Trust (Catholic)	2 Stars	40%	F
American Trust Allegiance (Christ. Science)	5 Stars	71%	D
Noah Fund (Christian)	4 Stars	55%	F
Timothy Plan Small Cap Value (Christian)	1 Star	100%	D
Timothy Plan Aggressive Growth	Not Rated	N/A	C
Timothy Plan Conservative Growth	Not Rated	N/A	C
Amana Trust Growth Fund (Islamic)	4 Stars	68%	F
Lutheran Brotherhood Fund (Lutheran)	3 Stars	37%	F
Lutheran Brotherhood Mid-Cap Growth	4 Stars	88%	A-
Lutheran Brotherhood Opportunity Growth	1 Star	100%	B
MMA Praxis Growth Fund (Mennonite)	Not Rated	52%	F
Christian Stewardship Fund	Not Rated	100%	A

ANALYSIS OF SPECIAL-ISSUE "SOCIALLY-RESPONSIBLE-SCREENED" MUTUAL FUNDS

Fund Name/Affiliation	Morningstar Quality Rating	% of Portfolio Is Clean	Overall Grade
Meyers Pride Value Fund (Pro-Gay)	3 Stars	28%	F
New Alternatives (Pro-Alternative Energy)	3 Stars	100%	B
DEM Fund (Pro-Minority Ownership)	Not Rated	97%	B
MFS Union Standard (Union Only)	2 Stars	45%	F
Victory Lakefront (Women & Minority)	2 Stars	20%	F
Women's Equity (Pro-Women's Equality)	3 Stars	40%	F

ANALYSIS OF STANDARD "SOCIALLY-RESPONSIBLE-SCREENED"
MUTUAL FUNDS

Fund Name/Affiliation	Morningstar Quality Rating	% of Portfolio Is Clean	Overall Grade
Ariel Appreciation Fund	3 Stars	95%	B+
Ariel Growth Fund	2 Stars	95%	B
Bridgeway Social Responsibility	5 Stars	53%	F
Calvert Social Investment Balanced	3 Stars	76%	D
Calvert Social Equity Fund	2 Stars	63%	F
Citizens Trust Emerging Growth	5 Stars	99%	A
Citizens Trust Global Equity	5 Stars	86%	B-
Citizens Trust Index	4 Stars	29%	F
Delaware Social Awareness	3 Stars	49%	F
Devcap Shared Return Fund	4 Stars	35%	F
Domini Social Equity Index Fund	4 Stars	31%	F
Dreyfus Premier Third Century Fund	4 Stars	46%	F
Flex Total Return Utilities	4 Stars	82%	C
Green Century Balanced Fund	5 Stars	85%	B-
Green Century Equity Fund	4 Stars	31%	F
Neuberger Berman Socially Responsive	2 Stars	36%	F
Parnassus Equity Income Fund	3 Stars	48%	F
Parnassus Fund	2 Stars	74%	D
Pax World Balanced Fund	4 Stars	77%	C-
Rightime Social Awareness Fund	1 Star	85%	C-
Security Social Awareness Fund	3 Stars	33%	F

ANALYSIS OF POPULAR MUTUAL FUNDS THAT SCREEN OUT
ONLY ALCOHOL AND TOBACCO

Fund Name/Affiliation	Morningstar* Quality Rating	% of Portfolio Is Clean	Overall Grade
AARP Growth & Income Fund	Not Rated	26%	F
AARP U.S. Stock Index Fund	4 Stars	39%	F
AARP Capital Growth	4 Stars	42%	F
American Fund's American Mutual	3 Stars	66%	F
American Fund's Washington Mutual	3 Stars	49%	F
Pioneer Fund	4 Stars	45%	F
Pioneer Balanced Fund	2 Stars	54%	F
Pioneer Equity Income Fund	3 Stars	38%	F
Pioneer II Fund	2 Stars	61%	F
Pioneer Mid-Cap Value	2 Stars	70%	D-

VALUES-BASED INVESTING SCREEN DEFINITIONS

Most values-based investing databases continue to offer the traditional three screens of alcohol, tobacco, and gambling. These screens are very black and white and have matured to a level of precision over many decades. These screens are held in common with traditional socially responsible investing. Screens that are unique to values-based investing can be defined as follows:

ABORTION

Companies are identified in this screen if they meet any of the following criteria:

- Any company that creates and distributes pharmaceutical products that are either specifically designed to be abortifacients or are used and promoted as abortifacients even if they have other medical uses as well.

---

*All references to Morningstar ratings and Clean ratings were accurate at the time of initial publication. This analysis is not intended to be used as solicitation to buy or analysis for investment purposes. For more information on the rate of return performance for each fund, please read its prospectus.

- Any company that creates and/or markets insurance policies that pay for elective abortions in states where they are not mandated by law.
- Any company that owns hospital or medical properties where elective abortions are completed.
- Any company that has for at least three consecutive years made a board-approved contribution to Planned Parenthood, non-profit population control group, or any other nonprofit pro-abortion advocacy group.

PORNOGRAPHY

Companies are identified in this screen if they meet any of the following criteria: companies that manufacture, create, and/or profit from any products that include pornography. Pornography is defined as the graphic, sexually explicit display of men, women, or children; as the graphic, sexually explicit subordination of women in pictures that also includes one of more of the following:

- Women are presented dehumanized as sexual objects, things, or commodities.
- Women are presented as sexual objects who enjoy pain or humiliation.
- Women are presented as sexual objects who experience sexual pleasure in being raped.
- Women are presented as sexual objects tied up, mutilated, bruised, or physically hurt in other ways.
- Women are presented in postures of sexual submission.
- Women are exhibited, such that women are reduced to those parts.
- Women are presented being penetrated by objects or animals.
- Women are presented in scenarios of degradation, injury, abasement, torture, shown as filthy or inferior, bleeding, bruised, or hurt in a context that makes these conditions sexual.

Anti-family Entertainment

Companies are identified in this screen if they meet any of the following criteria: companies that manufacture, create, and/or profit from any entertainment products that, while not meeting the guidelines of pornography, display partial nudity; discuss sexually explicit acts in nonmedical venues; promote casual heterosexual sex without consequences; promote incest, bestiality, pedophilia, or homosexual sex as healthy and legitimate lifestyles; display children in entertainment or advertisements in sexual innuendo or sexually suggestive displays; create public advertisements that represent heterosexual couples living together or homosexual partners as a legitimate alternative to heterosexual marriage; extremely vulgar language; extreme violence; any programming that desensitizes the viewer from the consequences of violence, murder or severe beating; suggestive eroticism in products aimed at teens or preteen consumers; or are blasphemous to Christian Scripture and doctrine.

Nonmarried Lifestyles

Companies are identified in this screen if they meet all of the following criteria:

- Companies that use shareholder money to pay for health and/or other employee benefits (so-called "domestic partner" benefits) for the nonmarried heterosexual or homosexual partners of employees.
- Companies that use shareholder money to create and market public advertisements that promote and represent nonmarried heterosexual or homosexual partners as legitimate and moral alternatives to heterosexual monogamous marriage.
- Companies that formally recognize and use shareholder money to subsidize internal gay and lesbian employee associations within their companies and/or subsidiaries.

Note: The nonmarried lifestyle screen is perhaps the most confusing and widely misunderstood of them all. The ultimate goal with this screen is to accurately identify those companies that go beyond a desire to promote employee equal opportunity, promote an atmosphere of diversity, or prevent expensive litigation. It is designed to find and identify those companies that choose to use shareholder money to actually promote an agenda within our culture that degrades the institution of traditional marriage by promoting nonmarried heterosexual live-in relationships and homosexual relationships as morally and socially equal to monogamous heterosexual marriage.

STANDARD SRI SCREEN DEFINITIONS

AN INVENTORY OF SRI AVOIDANCE SCREENS

The original three sin stock areas:

- Alcohol—companies that produce, market, or promote the use of alcoholic beverages.
- Tobacco—companies that produce tobacco products (more than 97 percent of all SRI managers include this screen).
- Gambling—companies that operate casinos or are suppliers of equipment used for lotteries and legal gambling.

OTHER AVOIDANCE SCREENS[1]

- Animal Rights—companies that kill or injure animals in the course of medical or product testing; raising animals for food under cruel living conditions; companies that contain animals in unnatural environments like zoos; or companies that abuse animals in the entertainment industry or for the sake of any other business activity.
- Environment, Global Warming—Companies that are producers of coal and oil; selected utility and transportation companies that use excessive fossil fuels; forestry companies; and any

companies that use great amounts of energy in manufacturing processes.

- Environment, Pollution, and Toxic Products—Companies whose industrial processes result in hazardous waste or water or air pollution; companies that are destructive to the "natural" environment; companies that produce pesticides, ozone-depleting chemicals, and certain plastics.
- Labor, Discrimination—Companies that do not offer equal opportunities to employees based on race, gender, national origin, religion, and sexual preference.
- Labor, Exploitation—Companies that exploit poor people through low wages and oppressive working conditions.
- Nuclear Power—Companies that operate nuclear power plants; companies that manufacture nuclear reactors or nuclear-related equipment.
- Repressive Regimes—Companies whose businesses support regimes that violate the human rights of their citizens. (This could include media censorship, environmental destruction, colonialism, or a ban on labor unions.)
- Weapons and the Military—Companies that manufacture weapons employed in either the national defense of the country or those intended for personal use; companies that are suppliers to weapon manufacturers.
- United States Treasury—SRI methodology will also screen out the use of United States Treasury bills, notes, or bonds because the investor money raised through these debt instruments inherently go into the federal budget from which Defense Department dollars are ultimately spent. SRI methodology recommends "agency" bonds with similar safety such as government agency mortgage bonds (Fannie Mae, Freddie Mac, Sallie Mae).

- Executive Pay—Companies that pay "excessive compensation" to company executives and that violate "economic justice" from their workers.
- Biotechnology—Companies that patent genetic traits from the DNA of indigenous peoples without compensation and without sensitivity to "cultural dilution."
- The Medical Industry in general—Companies in the medical field, pharmaceutical companies, and Western medicine in general are disrupting our natural abilities to fight disease or are intervening in a matter that is not ours to control. Companies in the medical field that value profits over the health of the poor.
- Resource Extraction—Companies that participate in logging, mining, fossil fuel extraction, and over-fishing.

AN INVENTORY OF AFFIRMATIVE SCREENS

- Quality of Products—Companies that have strong quality assurance programs for their products.
- Quality of Workplace—Companies that involve employees in decision making and that have strong union representation.
- Quality of Diversity—Companies that have boards of directors that include women and minorities. Companies that have "progressive policies toward gays and lesbians, such as provision for same-sex domestic partner benefits."[2]
- Quality of Community Participation—Companies that support housing and education programs.
- Quality of Environmental Practices—Companies whose products directly contribute to a cleaner environment such as those involved with recycling and renewable energy such as solar power, wind power, and hydrogen power.
- Clean Transportation—Companies that are developing electric powered vehicles.

- Tree Savers—Companies that make recyclable products or that use recycled products.
- Health Foods—Companies that grow, package, and market agriculture products (food, health products) grown on family farms without modern agricultural chemicals or efficient processing.
- Environmental Cleanup—Companies that clean up environmental hazards like leaking storage tanks, radioactive waste, oil spills, and other waste without incineration.
- Green Real Estate—Companies that are in the business of urban and rural real estate without the inefficient sprawl of modern American suburbs that require additional transportation needs and that chew up natural land.

RESOURCES

DATA ON PUBLIC COMPANIES

If you are searching for ways to get information on public companies for your own homework, or for finding names and addresses, the following are some valuable Web sites that offer free services.

- *Hoovers.* One of the best sites for finding out basic information on companies regarding their business, their competitors, whom to contact, and where to contact them. Many services are free. Additional information is available by subscription. www.hoovers.com
- *EDGAR Online.* EDGAR is a site that provides all the information from Securities and Exchange Commission filings on every public company. You can find a gold mine of information directly from this site. Some services are free. Additional information is available by subscription. www.edgar-online.com

- *Sedar.* Sedar provides quick and concise access to basic public company information for free.
  www.sedar.com
- *Free Annual Reports.* You can order a free copy of a company's annual report through this Web site. While annual reports are largely written with marketing in mind, you can learn a great deal of information about a company's values from them.
  www.prars.com
- *Corporate Information.* This site is great for getting additional information on public companies around the world as well as research.
  www.corporateinformation.com
- *Yahoo Index.* The search engine Yahoo has a valuable free tool that will get you information on thousands of public companies.
  http://biz.yahoo.com/i/
- *Wright Investments.* A site that few people know about has an incredible amount of information from Wright Investor Services. This free service provides a great deal of research on public companies around the world.
  http://profiles.wisi.com/profiles/Comsrch.htm

VALUES-BASED INVESTING RESEARCH

- The Investigator at Crosswalk.com—Find ratings on any public companies for free at Crosswalk.com, the world's largest Christian Internet site. Its tool, the Investigator, offers VBI reports of your choice based on the screens you tailor for your own needs. If you like, the Investigator will also automatically show you alternative investments that are clean. The site also keeps you up-to-date on the latest cultural news stories from around the country that involve publicly owned companies.
  http://money.crosswalk.com/investigator/

- Pro Vita Advisors—Tom Strohbar is president of this small organization, which he operates in his spare time. He has been one of the pioneers at researching pharmaceutical companies for their involvement in the manufacture of abortifacients. While abortifacient research is Pro Vita's specialty, it also provides some information on gambling and other abortion screens. http://members.aol.com/ProVitaAdv/
- STOPP (Stop Planned Parenthood)—This organization has much updated news and is the leading watchdog on Planned Parenthood across the United States. http://www.all.org/stopp

TOP CHRISTIAN FINANCIAL INVESTING WEB SITES

- *The Money Channel at Crosswalk.com.* Crosswalk.com's money channel offers you the best of Larry Burkett, including answers to more than one thousand questions he has had in all his radio show broadcasts. Free stock quotes, special insight into debt management from Bob Frank, and investment insight from Austin Pryor and Ron Blue are also available. Finally, the Money Channel is home to a comprehensive and free financial planning online program known as "Financial Passport" and the best values-based investing research available through the Investigator. www.crosswalk.com
- *Sound Mind Investing.* Austin Pryor has become the best-known expert on fundamental investment planning from a biblical perspective. Learn more of his insights at "SMI Now" on the Web. www.sminow.com
- *Crown Financial Ministries.* The merger of Crown Ministries led by Howard Dayton and Christian Financial Concepts created by Larry Burkett has resulted in Crown Financial Ministries. You can find a wealth of information on debt management, debt

relief, biblical perspectives on managing money, and archives of Larry Burkett's writing over the years.

www.cfcministry.org

- *No-Debt Living:* One of the best places on the Internet to get insights on how to make your financial dollars go further. Debt reduction strategies included with a foundation of stewardship and a biblical perspective. Managed by one of the best in the business, Bob Frank.

  www.nodebtnews.com

- *Cheapskate Monthly.* Mary Hunt is one of the best-recognized writers and authors about debt management. Hunt is founder and publisher of *Cheapskate Monthly,* a newsletter to encourage financial confidence and responsible spending.

  www.cheapskatemonthly.com

TOP FINANCIAL WEB SITES TO ASSIST IN YOUR FINANCIAL GOALS AND RESEARCH, FOR INDIVIDUAL INVESTORS

Here is a list of my fifteen favorite financial Web sites for assisting you in your personal financial programs. These sites all present news and information in a consistent fashion without any anti-family bias.

- www.cnbc.com
- www.fool.com
- www.thestreet.com
- www.economist.com
- www.smartmoney.com
- www.briefing.com
- www.individualinvestor.com
- www.marketwatch.com
- www.onmoney.com
- www.forbes.com
- www.wallstreetcity.com

- www.money.com
- www.investorguide.com
- www.stockpoint.com
- www.buyandhold.com

SAMPLE LETTERS

LETTER TO COMPANY'S DIRECTOR OF INVESTOR RELATIONS

Dear [name of investor relations director]:

As I analyze companies in which to invest my money, I must review a number of factors in choosing which one is right for my personal situation.

In that regard, I am writing to inform you that new information has come to my attention that leads me to avoid investing in [name of company]. It may surprise you also to learn that this new information has nothing to do with your historical record for investment rate of return.

I am joining a growing national movement of investors who consider the cultural value of the companies they invest in to be as important as the investment value they offer. According to new research that has come to my attention, your company is involved with products and/or policies that are unacceptable and culturally offensive to me.

After researching your company further, I have found that your company is involved in the business of pornography, abortion, or other anti-family products or policies. I have found alternative companies within your industry with equally attractive investment track records that pass the cultural screening tests.

I encourage you to consider changing the course of your company so that it represents both attractive earnings forecasts as well as traditional values in your core business. At that time, I will be happy to consider becoming an investor, and owner, in your company.

Sincerely,
[Your name]
[Your return mailing and E-mail addresses]

LETTER TO A MUTUAL FUND MANAGER

Dear [name of manager]:

As an investor shopping for the right mutual fund, I must review a number of factors in choosing which one is right for my personal needs and situation.

In that regard, I am writing to inform you that new information has come to my attention that leads me to avoid investing in [name of mutual fund]. It may surprise you also to learn that this new information has nothing to do with your historical record for investment rate of return.

I am joining a growing national movement of investors who consider the cultural value of the companies represented in their mutual fund to be as important as the investment value they offer. According to new research that has come to my attention, your portfolio has a level of ownership in certain companies that are culturally offensive to me, and that is unacceptable.

After researching your fund, I have found companies in your portfolio that are involved in the business of pornography, abortion, or other anti-family products or policies. After looking elsewhere, I have found alternative mutual funds with equally attractive investment track records that pass the cultural screening tests.

I encourage you to consider replacing these few companies with others that represent both attractive earnings forecasts as well as traditional values in their core business. At that time, I will be happy to consider returning to your mutual fund.

Sincerely,
[Your name]
[Your return mailing and E-mail addresses]

LETTER TO A COMPANY BENEFITS MANAGER

(This letter is designed for an employee of a company to send a request to the company benefits manager to add at least one mutual fund option within the company retirement plan or 401(k) plan that passes values-based investment screens.)

Dear [name of benefits manager]:

As a participant in the company retirement plan or 401(k) plan, shopping for the right mutual fund option, I review a number of factors in choosing which one is right for my personal needs and situation.

In that regard, I ask you to consider adding at least one mutual fund offering in our plan that filters out culturally offensive holdings. I am a part of a growing number of employees who consider the cultural value of the companies represented in their mutual funds to be as important as the investment value they offer. According to research that has come to my attention, none of the fund portfolios in our plan at the present time provide the opportunity to invest in a fund void of culturally offensive holdings.

Specifically, I have found companies in at least one fund portfolio that are involved in the business of pornography, abortion, or other anti-family products or policies. I also know that in most cases there are alternative mutual funds with equally attractive investment track records that pass cultural screening tests.

I encourage you to consider adding at least one new mutual fund option that represents both attractive earnings forecasts as well as traditional values in their core business. I would be happy to discuss this further with you at your convenience. Thank you very much for your consideration.

Sincerely,
[Your name]
[Your return mailing and E-mail addresses]

SAMPLE INVESTMENT POLICY STATEMENT (IPS) WITH A CULTURAL POLICY SECTION

This is an example of an investment policy statement for investment professionals who are responsible for managing money on behalf of a church, parachurch ministry, denomination, church college cash fund, endowment, foundation, retirement plan, or any other institutional portfolio. Each entity should use this sample as a model to customize a policy to fit its needs and to comply with state and local laws, regulations, and other policies concerning the investment of public funds.

I. Policy Statement

It is the policy of National Men's Fellowship [fictitious name for sample only], referred to as NMF, that the administration of its funds and the investment of those funds shall be handled as its highest trust. Investments shall be made in a manner that will provide the maximum security of principal invested through limitations and diversification while meeting the daily cash flow needs of NMF and conforming to all applicable policies for governing the investment of funds. The receipt of a market rate of return will be secondary to the requirements for safety and liquidity. It is the intent of NMF to be in complete compliance with all local, state, and federal laws. The earnings from investments will be used in a manner that best serves the interests of NMF.

II. Scope

This investment policy applies to all the financial assets and funds held by NMF. These funds are defined in the NMF Annual Financial Report (AFR) and include:

- General Fund
- Debt Service Fund
- Special Revenue Fund
- Capital Project Fund

and any new funds created by NMF unless specifically exempted by the board of directors and this policy.

III. Objectives and Strategy

It is the policy of NMF that all funds shall be managed and invested with five primary objectives: values-sensitivity, safety, liquidity, diversification, and yield. These objectives encompass:

Values Sensitivity

All financial assets of NMF that are invested in company stock will be consistent with values-based analysis as determined by the NMF cultural policy statement.

Safety of Principal

Safety of principal is a foremost objective of NMF. Investments of NMF shall be undertaken in a manner that seeks to insure the preservation of capital in the overall portfolio. To obtain this goal, diversification is required in the portfolio's composition. The suitability of each investment decision will be made on the basis of these objectives.

Liquidity

NMF's investment portfolio will remain sufficiently liquid to enable it to meet all operating requirements that might be reasonably anticipated.

Diversification

Diversification of the portfolio will include diversification by maturity, market sector, and the use of a number of broker/dealers for diversification and market coverage.

Yield

NMF's investment portfolio shall be designed with the objective of attaining a market rate of return throughout budgetary and economic cycles, taking into account NMF's risk constraints and the cash flow of the portfolio. "Market rate of return" may be defined as the average yield of the current three-month U.S. Treasury Bill or such other index that most closely matches the average maturity of the portfolio.

Effective cash management is recognized as essential to good fiscal management. Cash management is defined as the process of managing monies in order to ensure maximum cash availability. NMF shall maintain a comprehensive cash management program that includes collection of accounts receivable, prudent investment of its available cash, disbursement of payments in accordance with invoice terms, and the management of banking services.

IV. LEGAL LIMITATIONS, RESPONSIBILITIES, AND AUTHORITY

Direct specific investment parameters for the investment of non-profit funds in [state] are found in the [reference to statute]. These statutes are attached as Exhibit A.

In a situation in which the ministry or church has additional statutory requirements or charter requirements affecting investment, those references should also be made in this section.

V. DELEGATION OF INVESTMENT AUTHORITY

The chief financial officer [or treasurer, etc.], acting on behalf of the NMF board of directors, is designated as the investment officer of NMF and is responsible for investment management decisions and activities. The board is responsible for considering the quality and capability of staff, investment advisers, and consultants involved in investment management and procedures. All participants in the investment process shall seek to act responsibly as custodians of the ministry.

The investment officer shall develop and maintain written administrative procedures for the operation of the investment program consistent with this investment policy. Procedures will include reference to safekeeping, require and include master repurchase agreements, wire transfer agreements, banking services contracts, and other investment-related activities.

The administrative procedures are very important and should be reviewed annually. The auditors, or an internally designated individual, might review the investment process for compliance with this policy and those procedures.

The investment officer shall be responsible for all transactions undertaken and shall establish a system of controls to regulate the activities of subordinate officials and staff.

The investment officer shall designate a staff person as a liaison/deputy in the event that circumstances require timely action and the investment officer is not available.

No officer or designee may engage in an investment transaction except as provided under the terms of this policy and the procedures established by the investment officer and approved by the board of directors.

VI. PRUDENCE

The standard of prudence to be used in the investment function shall be the "prudent person" standard and shall be applied in the context of managing the overall portfolio. This standard states: "Investments shall be made with judgment and care, under circumstances then prevailing, which persons of prudence, discretion, and intelligence exercise in the management of their own affairs, not for speculation, but for investment, considering the probable safety of their capital as well as the expected income to be derived."

Limitation of Personal Liability

The investment officer and those delegated with investment authority under this policy, when acting in accordance with the written procedures and this policy and in accord with the prudent person rule, shall be relieved of personal responsibility and liability in the management of the portfolio.

The prudence of investment decisions should be based on the portfolio as a whole and not based upon the worth or history of a particular investment transaction. However, the statement of the prudent person standard is important to emphasize safety, and the limitation of liability assures that no one making the investment can be held personally liable for market changes. This does not relieve him of following the policy strictly.

VII. INTERNAL CONTROLS

The investment officer shall establish a system of written internal controls to be reviewed annually with the NMF board of directors. The controls shall be designed to prevent loss of ministry funds due to

fraud, employee error, misrepresentation by third parties, unantici-
pated market changes, or imprudent actions by employees of NMF.

Cash Flow Forecasting

Cash flow forecasting is designed to protect and sustain cash flow
requirements of NMF. Supplemental to the financial and budgetary
systems, the investment officer will maintain a cash flow forecasting
process designed to monitor and forecast cash positions for investment
purposes. Cash flow will include the historical researching and monitoring of specific cash flow items, payables, and receivables as well as
overall cash position and patterns.

VIII. AUTHORIZED INVESTMENTS

A. Cultural Policy Statement

All investment money in NMF will adopt values-based investment
screening tests to be accepted into any NMF equity-related investment
accounts. Companies that have products or policies that violate any of
the following values screens will not be authorized for purchase. The
investment officer will be responsible for the initial and regular analysis of all NMF equity holdings as they relate to the following values-
based screening criteria:

Alcohol—Companies are screened out if they manufacture alcoholic beverage products.

Tobacco—Companies are screened out if they manufacture any
tobacco consumer products, including cigarettes, cigars, pipe tobacco,
and/or chewing tobacco.

Gambling—Companies are screened out if they profit from gambling operations, the manufacturing of equipment specifically used in
gambling, or profit from contracting to outside gambling companies
to provide gambling services for their resort, hotel, or cruise properties.

Abortion—Companies are screened out if they meet any of the following criteria:

- Any company that creates and distributes pharmaceutical products that are either specifically designed to be abortifacients or are used and promoted as abortifacients even if they have other medical uses as well
- Any company that creates and/or markets insurance policies that pay for elective abortions in states where they are not mandated by law
- Any company that owns hospital or medical properties where elective abortions are completed
- Any company that has for at least three consecutive years made a board-approved contribution to Planned Parenthood, a nonprofit population control group, or any other nonprofit pro-abortion advocacy group

Pornography—Companies are screened out if they meet any of the following criteria: companies that manufacture, create, and/or profit from any products that include pornography. Pornography is defined as the graphic, sexually explicit display of men, women, or children; as the graphic, sexually explicit subordination of women in pictures that also includes one or more of the following: women are presented dehumanized as sexual objects, things, or commodities; or women are presented as sexual objects who enjoy pain or humiliation; or women are presented as sexual objects who experience sexual pleasure in being raped; or women are presented as sexual objects tied up, mutilated, bruised, or physically hurt in other ways; or women are presented in postures of sexual submission; or women are exhibited, such that women are reduced to those parts; or women are presented being penetrated by objects or animals; or women are presented in scenarios of degradation, injury, abasement, torture, shown as filthy or inferior, bleeding, bruised, or hurt in a context that makes these conditions sexual.

Anti-family Entertainment—Companies are screened out if they meet any of the following criteria: companies that manufacture, create, and/or profit from any entertainment products that, while not meeting the guidelines of pornography, display partial nudity; discuss sexually explicit acts in nonmedical venues; promote casual heterosexual sex without consequences; promote incest, bestiality, pedophilia, or homosexual sex as healthy and legitimate lifestyles; display children in entertainment or advertisements in sexual innuendo or sexually suggestive displays; create public advertisements that represent heterosexual couples living together or homosexual partners as a legitimate alternative to heterosexual marriage; extremely vulgar language; extreme violence; any programming that desensitizes the viewer from the consequences of violence, murder, or severe beating; suggestive eroticism in products aimed at teens or preteen consumers; or is blasphemous to Christian Scripture and doctrine.

Nonmarried Lifestyles—companies are screened out if they meet all of the following criteria:

- Companies that use shareholder money to pay for health and/or other employee benefits (so-called "domestic partner" benefits) for the nonmarried heterosexual or homosexual partners of employees
- Companies that use shareholder money to create and market public advertisements that promote and represent nonmarried heterosexual or homosexual partners as a legitimate and moral alternative to heterosexual monogamous marriage
- Companies that formally recognize and use shareholder money to subsidize internal gay and lesbian employee associations within their companies and/or subsidiaries

B. Authorized Investment Policy

Acceptable investments under this policy shall be limited to the instruments listed below. The investments are to be chosen in a manner that promotes values sensitivity, diversity of market sector, and maturity. The choice of high-grade government investments and high-grade money market instruments is designed to assure the marketability of those investments should liquidity needs arise.

- Obligations of the United States government, its agencies and instrumentalities, and government sponsoring enterprises, not to exceed two years to stated maturity.

- Fully insured or collateralized certificates of deposit from a bank domiciled in the state and under the terms of a written depository agreement with that bank, not to exceed one year to the stated maturity.

- Bankers acceptances not to exceed 180 days to stated maturity.

- Commercial paper rated A-1/P-1 or the equivalent by at least two nationally recognized rating agencies not to exceed 180 days to stated maturity.

- Repurchase agreements and reverse repurchase agreements not to exceed 180 days to stated maturity.

- No-load, SEC-registered money market funds, rated AAA, each approved specifically before use by the city council. No more than ___ percent of the entity's monthly average balance may be invested in money market funds.

- No-load, mutual funds registered with the SEC, investing exclusively in this policy's authorized investments. No more than ___ percent of the entity's monthly average balance may be invested in these funds.

- Equity investments of common stock, preferred stock, convertible stock that are traded on the New York Stock Exchange, the American Stock Exchange, or NASDAQ. No initial public offerings (IPOs) will be purchased using NMF funds.

IX. SAFEKEEPING AND COLLATERALIZATION

Prudent treasury management requires that all purchased securities be bought on a delivery versus payment basis and be held in safekeeping by either NMF, an independent third-party financial institution, or NMF's designated depository.

All safekeeping arrangements shall be designated by the investment officer and an agreement of the terms executed in writing. The third-party custodian shall be required to issue original safekeeping receipts to NMF, listing each specific security, rate, description, maturity, and cusip number. Each safekeeping receipt will be clearly marked that the security is held for NMF.

All securities pledged to NMF for certificates of deposit or demand deposits shall be held by an independent third-party bank. The safekeeping bank may not be within the same holding company as the bank from which the securities are pledged.

Collateralization

Collateralization shall be required on two types of investments:

- certificates of deposits over the FDIC insurance coverage of $100,000, and
- repurchase agreements.

In order to anticipate market changes and provide a level of additional security for all funds, the collateralization level required will be 102 percent of the market value of the principal and accrued interest.

Collateral will be of the following type securities only: The margin of 102 percent allows to the entity to prepare for any market price change during the term of the repo or CD. Both the master repo agreement and the depository agreement for purchase of CDs should stipulate who prices and how often the collateral should be priced. NMF may want to restrict collateral to securities that it prices itself from the financial press.

X. PERFORMANCE EVALUATION AND REPORTING

The investment officer shall submit monthly and annual reports to the NMF board of directors, containing sufficient information to permit an informed outside reader to evaluate the performance of the investment program. At a minimum, this report shall contain:

- Beginning and ending market value of the portfolio by market sector and total portfolio
- Beginning and ending book value of the portfolio by market sector and total portfolio
- Detail reporting on each asset (book, market, and maturity dates at a minimum)
- Overall current yield to maturity of the portfolio
- Overall weighted average maturity of the portfolio

XI. DEPOSITORIES

NMF will designate one banking institution through a competitive process as its central banking services provider at least every three years. This institution will be used for normal banking services, including disbursements, deposits, lockbox, and safekeeping of securities. Other banking institutions from which NMF may purchase certificates of deposit will also be designated after they provide their latest audited financial statements to the NMF board of directors.

XII. INVESTMENT POLICY ADOPTION BY THE BOARD OF DIRECTORS

NMF's investment policy shall be adopted by the board of directors. The policy shall be reviewed on an annual basis by the investment officer and the board of directors.

XIII. GLOSSARY

A glossary of financial terms used in this document is appended to this policy.

PRO-FAMILY RESOURCE GROUPS

To keep up on the cultural news today that may be impacting our families through corporate America tomorrow, it is helpful to know the leading advocacy groups. The following is a resource list of advocacy groups that are active in the same cultural issues that values-based investing revolves around.

American Conservative Union
38 Ivy St., SE
Washington, DC 20003
202-546-6555
www.conservative.org

American Family Foundation
Box 1170
Dunkirk, MD 20754
301-627-3346

American Life League, Inc.
P.O. Box 1350
Stafford, VA 22555
703-659-4171
703-659-2586 Fax
www.all.org

Center for Bioethical Reform
3855 E. La Palma Ave. #126
Anaheim, CA 92807
714-632-7520
1-800-959-9775
www.cbrinfo.org

Center for Pro-life Studies
P.O. Box 166
North Troy, VT 05859
802-988-4041

Christian Coalition
Attn: Pat Robertson
P.O. Box 1990
Chesapeake, VA 23320
800-325-4746
www.cc.org

Crusade for Life
18030 Bookhurst
Fountain Valley, CA 92708
714-963-4753

DeMoss Foundation
150 Radnor Cheester Rd.
St. Davids, PA 19087
215-254-5500

Eagle Forum
316 Pennsylvania Ave., SE
Washington, DC 20003
202-544-0353
www.eagleforum.org

Empower America
1776 First St., NW #900
Washington, DC 20006
800-332-2000
www.empower.org

Ethics and Public Policy Center
1015 15th St. SW, Suite 500
Washington, DC 20005
202-682-1200
www.eppc.org

Family Research Council
700 13th St. NW
Washington, DC 20005
202-393-2100

Family Resources Center
c/o Diocesan Respect Life Board
321 Main St.
Peoria, IL 61602
309-671-1550

Feminists for Life
733 15th Street, NW Suite 500
Washington, DC 20005
202-737-3352

The Firm Foundation
P.O. Box 9910
Chattanooga, TN 37412
615-499-0428

Fitch Fertility Center
6214 Rose Lake Ave
San Diego, CA 92119
619-466-1507
www.members.aol.com/tdececchi

Focus on the Family
8655 Explorer Drive
Colorado Springs, CO 80920
719-531-3400
719-531-3499 Fax
www.family.org

Free Congress Foundation
717 2nd St. NE
Washington, DC 20002
202-546-3000
800-446-3854
www.freecongress.org

Frontline Communications
1493 Palomar Dr.
San Marcos, CA 92069
619-737-9684

Heritage Foundation
214 Massachusetts Ave. NE
Washington, DC 20002
202-546-4400
www.heritage.org

Human Development Resource Council
3941 Holcomb Bridge Rd., Suite 300
Norcross, GA 30092
404-447-1598

Human Life Alliance
3570 Lexington Ave. North
Suite 205
St. Paul, MN 55726
651-484-1040
www.humanlife.org

Human Life Center
University of Steubenville
Steubenville, OH 43952
614-282-9935

Human Life Foundation
150 E. 35th St. #840
New York, NY 10016
212-685-5210

Libertarians for Life
13424 Hathaway Dr.
Wheaton, MD 20906
301-460-4141

Life Dynamics
P.O. Box 2226
Denton, TX 76202
940-380-8800
www.ldi.org

Life Issues Institute
1721 West Galbraith Rd.
Cincinnati, OH 45237
513-729-3600
www.lifeissues.org

Life Issues Television
818-566-3400

Life Matters Productions
P.O. Box 565
Lincoln Park, MI 48146

Life Network
17430 Campbell Road #206
Dallas, TX 75252
214-931-2273

Michael Fund
400 Penn Center Blvd., #721
Pittsburgh, PA 15235
412-823-6380

National Democrats for Life
1500 Massachusetts Ave. NW
Washington, DC 20005
202-463-0940

National Federation for Life
1011 First Ave.
New York, NY 10022
212-371-1000

National Life Center
686 N. Broad St.
Woodbury, NJ 08096
609-848-2380

National Right to Life Committee
419 7th St. NW, Suite 500
Washington, DC 20004
202-626-8823
www.nrlc.org

Project Truth
48 Dora Lane
Harrington Park, NJ 07640
201-569-3246

Pro-life Action League
6160 N. Cicero Ave. #600
Chicago, IL 60646
312-777-2900
www.prolifeaction.org

Republican National Coalition for Life
P.O. Box 618
Alton, IL 62002
618-462-4515
www.rnclife.org

**Republican National
Committee for Life**
Margaret D. Farley
1502 Haven Blvd.
Tampa, FL 33613
813-962-0531
813-960-0298 Fax

Seamless Garment Network
109 Pickwick Drive
Rochester, NY 14618
716-442-8497

**Taskforce of United Methodists
on Abortion & Sexuality
(TUMAS)**
512 Florence St.
Dothan, AL 36301
205-794-8543

Teachers Saving Children
P.O. Box 55103
Trenton, NJ 08638
609-298-4843

Traditional Values Coalition
139 C St. SE
Washington, DC 20003
202-223-6697
www.traditionalvalues.org

True Life Choice
4314 Edgewater Dr.
Orlando, FL 32804
407-294-4314
www.sparrow-finch.com/tlc/

U.S. Coalition for Life
P.O. Box 315
Export, PA 15632
412-327-7379

University Faculty for Life
Georgetown University
Box 2273
Washington, DC 20057
202-687-4208
202-687-5055 Fax

NOTES

CHAPTER 1

1. Speech, William Bennett, 1997 Conservative Political Action Conference, Omni Shoreham Hotel, Washington, D.C.

2. Speech, Charlton Heston, Harvard Law School Forum, 16 February 1999.

3. Charles Colson, *How Now Shall We Live?* (Wheaton, Ill.: Tyndale House, 1999), 17.

4. "Clinton Slams Violent Images," *Rocky Mountain News,* 11 May 1999.

5. "Senators told of link between violence, video games," CNN.com, 22 March 2000.

6. Ibid.

7. id Software corporate Web site, www.idsoftware.com.

8. Frank Lantz, *Ctheory Journal,* www.ctheory.com.

9. Testimony, Sabrina Steger, United States Senate Commerce Committee, 21 March 2000.

10. Interview, Hillary Rodham Clinton, "I Worry about Television," *Parade,* 11 April 1993.

11. Cal Thomas and Ed Dobson, *Blinded by Might: Why the Religious Right Can't Save America* (Grand Rapids, Mich.: Zondervan, 2000), 44.

12. Francis Schaeffer, *The Great Evangelical Disaster* (Wheaton, Ill.: Good News Publishers, 1984).

13. Terry Mattingly, "On Religion" column, 5 May 1999.

CHAPTER 2

1. "U.S. Supreme Court opinion—Dred Scott vs. Sanford," Chief Justice Roger B. Taney, 6 March 1857.

2. Ralph Reed, *Active Faith: How Christians Are Changing the Face of American Politics* (New York: Free Press, 1996), 109.

3. Ibid., 12.

4. Bob Dole, editorial, Daily Sentinel, 8 August 1996.

5. Keynote speech, Dr. James Dobson, Council for National Policy meeting, February 1998.

6. Cal Thomas and Ed Dobson, *Blinded by Might: Why the Religious Right Can't Save America* (Grand Rapids, Mich.: Zondervan, 2000), 14.

7. Cal Thomas, "Have We Settled For Caesar?", *Christianity Today*, 6 September 1999, 48.

8. Thomas and Dobson, *Blinded by Might*, 23.

9. Reed, *Active Faith*, 267.

CHAPTER 3

1. Charles Colson, *How Now Shall We Live?* (Wheaton, Ill.: Tyndale House, 1999), 13.

2. Cal Thomas and Ed Dobson, *Blinded by Might: Why the Religious Right Can't Save America* (Grand Rapids, Mich.: Zondervan, 2000), 44.

3. Ibid., 147.

CHAPTER 4

1. Transcript, XFL press conference, Vince McMahon, 3 February 2000.

2. Hoover's Business Reports Online, www.hoovers.com.

CHAPTER 5

1. "About the NYSE," www.nyse.com.

2. Press release, Telescan and Playboy Enterprises, 14 June 1999.

3. "Telocity Names Christie Hefner to Board of Directors," *Business Wire*, 20 April 2000.

4. "NASDAQ Reluctantly Embraces Topless-Bar Stock," *Wall Street Journal*, 8 August 1995.

5. Company report, Hoovers Business Directory Online, www.hoovers.com.

6. Ibid.

7. "WWF Keeps USA on Top of Cable Heap," *Variety*, 29 March 2000.

8. "GFN 50," Gay Financial Network, www.gfn.com.

9. "Big Companies are Openly Courting Gay Consumers," *Los Angeles Times*, 18 May 1999.

10. "Patterns of Corporate Philanthropy," Capital Research Center.

11. Hoovers Company Reports Online, www.hoovers.com.

12. Perucci Ferraiuolo, *Disney and the Bible: A Scriptural Critique of the Magic Kingdom* (Camp Hill, Pa.: Horizon Books, 1996), 72.

13. Peter and Rochelle Schweizer, *Disney: The Mouse Betrayed* (Washington, D. C.: Regnery, 1998), 112.

14. Press release, "GFN.com salutes most influential execs," 6 December 1999.

15. Ed Micken, "The 100 Best Companies for Gays and Lesbians," 1994.

16. Press release, GLAAD, "11th annual GLAAD Media Awards," 15 April 2000.

17. "About the NYSE," www.nyse.com.

CHAPTER 6

1. Press release, "AMA calls for divestment of all tobacco stocks and mutual funds," American Medical Association, 23 April 1998.

2. Press release, "CalPERS Votes No on Marriott Proposal #1," CalPERS, 12 March 1998.

3. Press release, "Big Disney Stockholder Urges More Independence for Board," 15 January 1998.

4. "Proxy Efforts Focus on Board Independence and Removal of Anti-Takeover Devices," May 2000.

5. Bob Briner, *Final Roar* (Nashville, Tenn.: Broadman & Holman Publishers, 2000).

CHAPTER 7

1. Morningstar Report, Gabelli Asset Fund, 31 May 2000.

2. Mary Naber, "Will values-based investing affect your returns?," Crosswalk.com, 1998.

3. Ibid.

4. Mary Naber, "VBI Part 2: Tangible Evidence," Crosswalk.com 1998.

5. Amy Domini and Peter D. Kinder, *Ethical Investing* (New York: Addison-Wesley, 1984).

6. Hal Brill, Jack A. Brill, and Cliff Feigenbaum, *Investing with Your Values: Making Money and Making a Difference* (Princeton, N.J.: Bloomberg Press, 1999), 53.

7. Company statistics, Domini Social Investments, 31 March 2000.

8. Thomas Van Dyck, letter to the editor, *Mutual Funds,* November 1997, 15.

CHAPTER 8

1. Hal Brill, Jack A. Brill, and Cliff Feigenbaum, *Investing with Your Values: Making Money and Making a Difference* (Princeton, N.J.: Bloomberg Press, 1999), 36.

2. Lawrence Ladd, "Social Responsible Investing," Unitarian Universalist Church, 2000 General Assembly.

3. *Christianity Today,* 26 April 1963.

4. "National Radio Pulpit," 7 November 1965.

5. Harold Martin, "What About the National Council of Churches?," Volume 2, Number 1, 1967.

6. Carl Henry, editorial, *Christianity Today,* 15 February 1963.

7. Pamphlet, Co-Op America, Statement of Mission, 1994.

8. "Eco-Nomics Made Simple," *Time,* 15 November 1999.

9. Press release, Social Investment Forum, 4 November 1999.

10. Rosemary Brown, Co-Op America, Socially Responsible Investing Mission, 1995.

11. Interfaith Center for Corporate Responsibility Web site, www.ic.org, 10 September 2000.

12. Brills and Feigenbaum, *Investing with Your Values,* 290–93.

13. Charles Colson, *How Now Shall We Live?* (Wheaton, Ill.: Tyndale House, 1999), 52.

14. Ibid., 55.

15. Susan DeFord, "Challenging the Corporate Conscience," *Washington Post,* 6 July 1996.

16. Cynthia Mayer, "Mutual Funds for the Socially Conservative," *Philadelphia Inquirer,* 29 September 1996.

17. Carole Gould, "Screening from the Right," *New York Times,* 27 October 1996.

18. MMA Praxis Mutual Funds Philosophy, MMA Web site, www.mma-online.org.

19. "Stewardship Solutions," MMA Praxis Mutual Funds Web site, www.mma-online.org.

20. "Mixing Business and Faith," CNNfn, 2 April 1999.

CHAPTER 9

1. *New York Times.*

2. "How to Boycott the Walt Disney Company," American Family Association, 8 December 2000, http://www.afa.net/disney/howto.asp.

CHAPTER 10

1. *Wall Street Journal*, 5 June 1995.

2. "Some Firms re-examine Giving to Boy Scouts," *The Charlotte Observer*, 29 August 2000.

3. Gerald Levin, guest opinion, *USA Today*, 12 March 1992.

4. Keynote speech, Bill Bennett, Conservative Political Action Conference, January 1996.

5. *Wall Street Journal* article, 12 June 1995.

6. Richard Zoglin, "A Company Under Fire," *Time*, 12 June 1995.

7. Don Feder, syndicated column, *Boston Herald*, 7 June 1995.

8. Senator Bob Dole, speech transcript, 20th Century Fox studios, Los Angeles, 31 May 1995.

9. John Leo, column, *U.S. News & World Report*, March 1995.

10. Time Warner Annual Report, 1994.

11. Zoglin, "A Company Under Fire."

12. Ibid.

13. Farrell Kramer, "Time Warner feels the heat, drops gangsta rap," Associated Press, 28 September 1995.

14. Chris Sicks, "Omni Hotels: doing the right thing," Crosswalk.com, 4 January 2000.

15. Ibid.

16. *Business Week*, "Planned Parenthood Didn't Plan on This," 1990.

17. Mary Naber, "Influencing Corporate America," Crosswalk.com.

18. Nancy Benac, "U.S. abortion foes help prevent RU-486 production," *Seattle Times*, 19 July 1998.

CHAPTER 11

1. "CBS Fight a Litmus Test for Conservatives," *Washington Post*, 31 March 1985, 1.

2. Ibid.

3. Anitha Reddy, "Soldiers for the Shareholder," *The Washington Post*, 27 August 2000, H1.

4. Ibid.

5. Ibid.

6. "News of the Bible from Bible Society," Bible Society Web site, www.biblesociety.org.uk.

7. Gary Moore, *Ten Golden Rules for Financial Success* (Grand Rapids, Mich.: Zondervan, 1997).

8. Gary Moore, "Spiritual Investing" speech, "Making a Profit While Making a Difference Conference," 11 May 2000.

CHAPTER 12

1. Charles Colson, *How Now Shall We Live?* (Wheaton, Ill.: Tyndale House, 1999), 25.

2. Ibid.

3. Press Secretary Joe Lockhart, "White House Press Briefing Transcript," 16 December 1999.

4. Francis Schaeffer, "A Christian Manifesto" speech transcript, Coral Ridge Presbyterian Church, 1982.

5. Jane and Craig Parshall, *The Light in the City: Christians Must Advance and Not Retreat* (Nashville, Tenn.: Thomas Nelson, 2000), 113.

6. "Ask Larry, Questions and Answers from Larry Burkett," Crosswalk.com Money Channel, www.crosswalk.com/cfc/articles.

7. Bob Briner, *Roaring Lambs: A Gentle Plan to Radically Change Your World* (Grand Rapids, Mich.: Zondervan Publishing House, 2000), 28, 30.

CHAPTER 13

1. William Bennett, *The Index of Leading Cultural Indicators: American Society at the End of the 20th Century* (Waterbrook Press, 2000), 10.

2. Daniel D. Busby, Kent E. Barber, and Robert L. Temple, *The Christian's Guide to Worry-free Money Management: Ten Easy Steps*, 1.

APPENDIX

1. Hal Brill, Jack A. Brill, and Cliff Feigenbaum, *Investing with Your Values: Making Money and Making a Difference* (Princeton, N.J.: Bloomberg Press, 1999), 79–118.

2. Ibid., 97.